ISBN: 9781313393805

Published by:
HardPress Publishing
8345 NW 66TH ST #2561
MIAMI FL 33166-2626

Email: info@hardpress.net
Web: http://www.hardpress.net

Remains of Nithsdale and Galloway Song.

REMAINS

OF

NITHSDALE AND GALLOWAY

SONG.

BY

R. H. CROMEK, F.A.S., Ed.,

Editor of 'The Reliques of Robert Burns.'

———— ✦ ————

PAISLEY: ALEXANDER GARDNER.

1880.

NOTE.

THE re-issue of CROMEK's "Remains of Nithsdale and Galloway Song" is justified rather by the rarity of the work, its interesting pictures of local manners, and the circumstances in which it was written, than by its claims to bear the name assigned to it by the Editor. No doubt there are contained in it many snatches of old songs, but these are treasured as flies in amber, and bear but a small proportion to the other portions of the volume. The book owes more to Allan Cunningham than to tradition, and it is difficult to understand how far the English Editor was sincere in recording his belief that he was giving to the world a genuine collection of unpublished Nithsdale and Galloway Song. That Cunningham was the author of nearly all the pieces in the Collection there cannot be a reasonable doubt, and whether CROMEK was so thoroughly hoaxed as his statements would imply, may be doubted. Apart, however, from its doubtful antiquarian claims, the volume is interesting as the production of a representative Scotsman, whose songs are at least founded on ballad and traditionary lore, and whose expositions of the manners and customs of the peasantry of his native district, embodied in the work, are replete with information which every antiquarian must prize.

ROBERT CROMEK, an engraver by trade, was a native of Yorkshire. He early became an enthusiastic student of ballad poetry, and interested himself in following up relics of the songs and manners of the past. When the songs of Burns were given to the world, he was so attracted by their delineations of Scottish life, that he made a pilgrimage to the North, and collected material for his "Reliques of Robert Burns," which he published in 1808, and for which he was made a member of the Antiquarian Society of Edinburgh. After its publication he again visited Scotland, and it was during his second visit that he met Allan Cunningham, and secured the material which appears in the Nithsdale and Galloway Remains. Cunningham was at the time working as a mason in Dumfriesshire, but neglected his trade in his ardent pursuit of literature; and it was partly through CROMEK's advice and influence, that in the very year when the "Remains" appeared, he went to London, and became connected with the newspaper press. It is said that Allan presented some of his poetry to CROMEK, but received only feeble praise for his productions, until the thought occurred to him that he might secure more favourable criticisms if he appealed to CROMEK's weak side, by saying they were traditionary remains. The bait took, the patron became enthusiastic, and the result was "The Remains of Nithsdale and Galloway Song."

CROMEK died in London in 1812. His memory deserves the gratitude of Scotsmen. Though a native of the South, he gave his whole heart to the study of Scottish tradition, and his work is well worthy of being preserved. On the whole, it is probable that he really believed the representations made to him as to the nature of the poetry he published as "Remains," and that Cunningham was the perpetrator of a hoax such as has been repeatedly imposed upon enthusiastic men of letters.

REMAINS

OF

NITHSDALE AND GALLOWAY SONG:

WITH

HISTORICAL AND TRADITIONAL NOTICES

RELATIVE TO THE

MANNERS AND CUSTOMS OF THE PEASANTRY.

NOW FIRST PUBLISHED BY

R. H. CROMEK, F.A.S. Ed.

EDITOR OF 'THE RELIQUES OF ROBERT BURNS.'

' ——— a faithful portrait, unadorned,
Of manners lingering yet in Scotia's vales.'

LONDON:

PRINTED FOR T. CADELL AND W. DAVIES, STRAND,

By T. BENSLEY, Bolt Court, Fleet Street.

1810.

M r s. *C O P L A N D ,*

AT length, my dear Madam, the grateful task in which I engaged, is performed. You well know with what anxiety I undertook my humble share in this Work, and how much your kind assistance smoothed my path, and your cheering approbation encouraged me to appear for a second time, before a less indulgent tribunal. What its decision may be I cannot anticipate—I respect the censures of good men, and to their favourable acceptance I submit my labours.

R. H. CROMEK.

London,
64, Newman Street, 1810.

CONTENTS.

CLASS III.

JACOBITE BALLADS, 1715.

JACOBITE BALLADS, 1745.

CLASS IV.

OLD BALLADS AND FRAGMENTS.

APPENDIX.

The Design on the Title-Page is engraved on Wood, by CLENNELL, from the pencil of STOTHARD. It represents an Old Woman communicating to Lord Nithsdale's Tenants the news of his Escape to France. Vide p. 112.

INTRODUCTION.

THE Scottish poets have raised a glorious fabric of characteristic Lyric, the fairest perhaps any nation can boast. The foundations were laid by various unknown hands, and even of those who raised the superstructure few have attained the honour of renown; but the whole has been reformed and completed by a man whose fame will be immortal as his genius was transcendant. The name of ROBERT BURNS, let a Scotchman pronounce it with reverence and affection! He produced the most simple and beautiful lyrics himself; he purified and washed from their olden stains many of the most exquisite of past ages. He collected others with all the glowing enthusiasm of an antiquary, and with the keen eye of an exquisite critic and poet. It was on these beautiful old ballads and songs that BURNS laid the foundation of his greatness. Their simplicity he copied; he equalled their humour, and excelled their pathos. But that flame which they helped to raise absorbed them in its superior brightness; so that the more we investigate

the sources from which he drew, the more our reverence
for his genius is increased. Whatever he transplanted
grew up and flourished with a vigour unknown in the
parent soil; whatever he imitated sinks almost into
insignificance placed by the side of the imitation. He
rolls along like a mighty river, in the contemplation of
which the scattered streams that contribute to its greatness
are forgotten.

It has been the work of the present collector to redeem
some of those fine old songs, overshadowed by the genius
of BURNS; such especially as have never before been
published, and are floating in the breath of popular
tradition.

Many of these are peculiar to certain districts of Scotland, and tracts of finely situated country. Deeply
founded in the manners and customs of the peasantry,
they keep hold of their minds, and pass from generation
to generation by these local ties :—their flashes of broad
humour, their vivid description render them popular;
and their strong touches of native feeling and sensibility
make a lasting impression on the heart.

It is worthy of remark, that in no district of England
are to be found specimens of this simple and rustic poetry.
The influence of commerce has gradually altered the
character of the people : by creating new interests and
new pursuits, it has weakened that strong attachment to
the soil which gives interest to the localities of popular

ballads, and has destroyed those cherished remembrances of former times which impart to a rude and unpolished strain, all the pathos of the most laboured elegy.

We may safely premise, that many of the most valuable traditional songs and ballads perished in those afflicting times of reformation and bloodshed which belong to Queen Mary, to Charles, and to James. A great change then took place in the Scottish character :—the glowing vivacity and lightsomeness of the Caledonian Muses were quenched in the gloomy severity of sour fanatic enthusiasm, and iron-featured bigotry. The profanity of Song was denounced from the pulpit, and the holy lips of Calvinism would not suffer pollution by its touch. Dancing, to which it is nearly allied, was publicly rebuked, attired in fornicator's sackcloth. The innocent simplicity and airiness of Song gave way to holier emanations ; to spiritualized ditties, and to the edifying cadence of religious, reforming cant. Such seems to have been the state of Song when ALLAN RAMSAY arose. His beautiful collections rekindled the smothered embers of Lyric Poetry—but he could not redeem the lost treasures of past ages; nor rake from the ashes of the fallen religion the sacred reliques of its songs. A few were redeemed—but they were trimmed anew, and laced with the golden thread of metaphysic foppery, over the coarse and homely hoddin gray of rural industry. Their naïveté of feeling—their humour and amiable simplicity, now gave way to the gilded and varnished trappings and tassel-ings of courtly refinement.

Scottish humour attempted to smear his thistles with the oil and balm of polite satire, till they lost their native pungency. Love was polished aud boarding-schooled, till the rough mint-stamp of nature was furbished off it. The peasantry, however, preserved in their traditional songs and ballads a fair portion of the spirit and rough nature of the olden times. To the peasantry the Scotch are indebted for many of their most exquisite composi-tions. Their judgment in the selection and preservation of song scarcely can be sufficiently appreciated : *Barbour's* Bruce; *Blind Harry's* Sir William Wallace ; *Ramsay's* original works, and his *Collections of Songs ;—Fergusson,* and *Burns* are to be found in every Scottish hamlet, and in every hand. Accompanying these, there are a multi-tude of songs, ballads, and fragments which descend by tradition, and are early imprinted on every mind ;—

> "Which spinners and the knitters in the sun,
> · And the free maids, that weave their thread with bones,
> Do use to chant of."

The language of Scotland is peculiarly fitting, pliant, and compressive for all the sweet civilities of affection. There is a creamy softness in the rustic Doric which would almost convince one that it had been at first fashioned for the familiar fervency of love. It is peculiarly adapted to express tenderness and humour, as the songs of BURNS exquisitely prove.

It was once the opinion of BURNS that a poet of a nice ear, and fine taste, might compose songs without the encumbrance of rhyme.* He was led into this error by the seeming dissonance of many of them in this necessary appendage. These jarring rhymes are, however, softened into similarity of sound when they are sung. This is to a critical observer the evident stamp of *Rusticity*, and is not to be found in the compositions of the elegant and the learned.

To me it appears, from the glowing warmth and energy of their composition, that these songs are the production of the peasantry. The hurried and negligent hand of rusticity is plain upon them. Their familiar manner— their close reference to the imagery and occupations of rural affairs, and to rustic incidents, point forcibly to the source from whence they sprung. Many of these rude and abrupt effusions are more touching than if they were elegantly planned out. The broken agitation of feeling, mingled with the plaintive speech of desolate woe, naturally vents itself in those spontaneous bursts of passion and sentiment which savour of a distempered mind and a broken heart.

---

* "Reliques of Burns." p. 347.

At the close of the Rebellion in 1745, the Scottish rustic character arose from the wrecks of feudal juris- diction. The peasantry had been silently preparing and modelling their minds for emancipation ever since the Revolution of 1688. The Legislature, by a strange fatality, neglected to bestow political liberty with freedom of conscience. The English Council evidently looked on them as a horde of naked wretches dwelling in hovels in the fag-end of Creation ; nor did the hurried attempt of Mar, in 1715, raise them any higher in public estima- tion.

But the wild and daring schemes of Prince Charles, in 1745, compelled the Government to look to the North with consternation. They beheld with terror and dismay a few thousands of half-armed rustics making their way through disciplined legions, and drawing their swords within an hundred miles of the capital. After signal acts of barbarity, peace was again restored, and the Legislature took serious measures to amend the condition of Scotland. The hereditary power of the chieftains was broken, and the common people were delivered from the yoke of vassalage. Scotland then assumed a new and distinct character. Her inland peasantry, removed from the bustle and contamination of foreign commerce, still preserved that perfect in- dividuality of character which had been forming itself ever since the Reformation. The petty chieftains were now no longer formidable to Government, nor to their vassals. They beheld with indignation the pillars of their sovereignty cast down. Proud of ancestorial achievements, they abandoned their wonted affability and gentleness, and disdained to mingle with their former dependants, now equally free and aspiring with themselves. From this change we may date the immense distance, still maintained in Scotland, between the lord of the manor and his cottager.

The peasantry, with the zeal of newly-recovered freedom, began to occupy a station in the annals of industry. Taught by their fathers to regard every foreign fashion as a dangerous innovation, they preserved themselves unpolluted with the stream of refinement which was sapping the ancient manners and character of their nobility and chieftains. France, their old ally and relation, had closed up one source of pollution by drawing the sword against them. Their sister England was still regarded with a stern suspicious eye. The cruel persecutions of the English Church—the murders of Glencoe—and the bloody underhand policy against their favourite Settlement on the Isthmus of Darien, did not serve to mitigate the stern counsels of rival and national prejudice. Thus they received the refinement and manners of England with the same aversion as they did her invading armies of former times, who came to conquer and enslave. This hatred their national poetry, their traditional history,—and their religious writings, still preserve and inculcate.   Almost all their poetry, from the venerable song of Barbour, down to the Heroic Welcome of the Brus of Bannock-burn, by Burns, stir up and cherish the embers of former broil.   Their volumes of the martyred worthies, written in the bitterness of persecuting contest with English pre-lacy, threw religion into the scale of political hatred, and strengthened their prejudices against their southern brethren.

The fountains of foreign instruction being thus sealed against them, they applied themselves to their own resources, and stored their minds with the written and traditionary histories of their native land.   These were related by the old persons, or read by the younger, at every fire-side, during the winter evenings, and in the leisure hours of labour, or while tending their flocks. The condition of the inland peasantry was easy, and comparatively affluent.   Almost every one had a cow, and a few acres of land.   Oatmeal, pease, delicate mutton, fish in every stream, and milk and butter, fur-nished the necessaries and some of the dainties of exist-ence.   Their clothes were all of home manufacture. The men's dress was mostly a fine mixed gray, from wool of natural dye—a large chequered plaid and bonnet—their shoes were formed of leather tanned by the shoe-maker; the women's gowns were of lint and woollen, fancifully mixed, and frequently of exquisite fineness, which is still a popular and becoming dress. From their schools, of which there are two or three in every parish, they learned to read and write. Having found means of gratifying their insatiable thirst after knowledge, every book was to them a source of pleasure ; and so eager was the pursuit, that there are many persons among them who have on their memory the rhymed exploits of Wallace, the popular parts of Barbour, Ramsay's Gentle Shepherd, and most of his original and collected songs, with many pieces of beautiful and fugitive poetry recorded by their fathers. Add to these the Psalms of David, and many of the finest chapters of our translated Bible. From their fathers and from their ministers they learned to contemplate the sacred 'mysteries of the Bible with submissive veneration. Unskilled in the figurative language of poetic instruction, or lost in the raptured soarings and sublimities of historic inspiration, they took poetic licence for truth, and the wild, unbridled flights of Eastern personification were the revelation of Heaven, written with the finger of the Deity. The Bible was put into every youthful hand, with "*This is the hand-writing of God.*" Every sentence was taken as it is written in the close fidelity of translation. Hence arose that superstitious belief in wizards, witches, and familiar spirits, the popular creed of heathenism.* The Cottars devoutly opened

---

* Perhaps natural taste and reason will never be able to banish these phantoms

b

the book of God every evening, and on every Sabbath
morning, to offer thanksgivings and praises, and to
instruct and admonish their children.   The holy Songs
of David were committed to memory to be allied to the
church melodies.   The mind received from these a cast
and impressure of thoughtful melancholy, which often
exalts it to the noblest conceptions.   A rigid moral
austerity, and severity of religious conversation, were
the consequences of their long struggles with English
supremacy, and formed no part of their natural constitution ; on the contrary, they were ever ready to mingle
in the pleasant mirth of society.   Their ancient music
still lingered among them, a proscribed fugitive of
religious zeal : wedded to those old Songs and ballads,
the favourites of every age, it was beyond the power of
banishment.   This love of music and poetry was pri-
vately fostered by the old men and women.   It had
been their own delight and amusement, and they loved
to cherish the fond remembrance of other years.   They
appointed meetings at each other's houses for dancing

---

from a Scottish mind. To this day many of the good old people of Galloway
thus turn the sacred denunciation of prophecy against sceptics and emendators:
   " For I testify unto every man that heareth the words of the prophecy of this
" book, If any man shall add unto these things, God shall add unto him the
" plagues that are written in this book : And if any man shall take away from the
" words of the book of this prophecy, God shall take away his part out of the book
" of life, and out of the holy city."—REV. xxii. 18, 19.

and singing, to which, at the close of day-toil, the lads and lasses would hasten for several miles round. Here they sung, accompanied by the violin or lowland pipe. The old men recounted the exploits and religious struggles of their ancestors, and mingled in the song, or joined in the dance.

Enraptured with their music, and emulous of praise, the youths cultivated those seeds of poesy which are more or less to be found in every lover's heart. In the presence of those whom they loved, they strove to excel in the strains of tender complaint or pathetic appeal, which were sung and so much admired by their mistresses. Inspired with such sensations, they caught up the prominent features of their adventures, and sung of their jealousies and wooing felicities, in numbers worthy of remembrance. To the heart of a Scottish peasant it is a sensation of divine rapture to listen and behold his beloved lass warble, and sweetly modulate those strains to which her tender heart and beautiful face had imparted sympathetic loveliness. The interview at some favourite secluded thorn, in the dew of gloaming; the stolen looks of love; the midnight meeting of chaste affection; the secret kiss and unheard whisper in the dancings and trystes, are the favourite themes of poetic record. These songs were sung before the aged; and their praise, with the kind looks of approval from their mistresses, was a reward sufficient to stimulate to nobler

exertion.   Old songs were altered to suit some more
recent occurrence ; their language was frequently minted
anew, and the song would take a novel appearance from
a small incident of love, or a gallant exploit.

To these public dancing trystes the daughters of the
chieftains would sometimes go in peasants' disguise ;
possibly to partake in the rural felicities of unrestrained
gaiety and frolic, or, perhaps, smitten with the charms of
some young peasant, they wished to listen to the natural
eloquence of love, and the fervent pathos of rustic wooing.   There are yet some remnants of songs which
evidently allude to rencounters of this kind, and many
more might, perhaps, have been collected on a more
diligent search.

The language of the peasantry has none of that vulgar
broadness so disgusting in those sea-coast towns which
commerce has corrupted.   Imagery, drawn from the
select resources of nature, will clothe itself in chaste and
becoming language : the summer wind—the gloaming
dewfall among the loose locks of a lovely maiden—the
flower-tops bent with dew—the balmy smell of the
woods—the honey-combs of the wild bee—afford fine
poetic figures, which nought but profligacy can pollute
or misapply.   The crimson brook-rose, the yellow-
freckled lily, the red-lipped gowan, the pale primrose,
the mealy cowslip, the imbedding thyme, are flourishing
in rustic pastoral ;—and the rich scented hawthorn, the

honey-leafed oak, the tasseling honey-suckle, and the
bloomy promise of the orchards and bean fields, embalm
themselves in song, as pure as the dew which the hand
of evening drops on them. But the tender eloquence
of the new-paired birds, and the infant song of the new-
flown nestlings were happily caught by peasant discern-
ment :

> "The new-paired laverocs among the blooming howes,
> Sing kindlie to my Mary while she ca's home the ewes."

The lark is a chief favourite ; and being the herald of
morning, sings over head to the swain returning from the
errands of love, who naturally puts his own felicities
in her mouth. The wild and mellow mavis, the loud-
lilting blackbird, the familiar rose-linnet, the lively gold-
spink, are all classical songsters, whose warblings are
pleasing to a lover's ear. From the sacred pages of the
Bible the peasantry drew many of their finest ideas and
imagery. It imparted a tone of solemn sincerity to the
promises of love, and gave them a more popular currency
among the aged and decorous. Another source of instruction, was the select code of Proverbs which wisdom
had stored up in the progress of society : these, being
short and happily figurative, were the current coin of
primitive converse.

Owing to the great distance between the chieftain and

cottar these productions never passed into the notice of the great. Composed and sung in unaspiring obscurity, their authors never attempted to hold them up to public notice. The applause at a country wedding, at a kirn dancing, at a kirk supper, after a bridal, satisfied the bard's vanity : and, perhaps, the secret assurance that his sweetheart would live in his verses among her great grand-children, was the utmost bound of his ambition. The Scottish peasantry have within these dozen years completely overturned their ancient customs. The hurrying progress of agriculture, with the load of taxes, call for heavier labours than the evening dance, or the gaieties of song; yet still they possess much of that romantic spirit of love-adventure and intrigue which the chivalrous feats of knight-errantry amours had sown among them. There is a noble daringness, and an aspiring stretch of mind in many of the lowly rustics which might grace a princely cavalier of the days of feudal adventure. Love songs are early imprinted on every mind, and music accompanies them. Nothing, then, is required to make a poetic peasant, but to have his heart warmly touched with the virgin-fingers of love. Careless and unknowing of any fame beyond his mistress's will and approval, he writes from his heart and soul ! He writes love as he feels it ; and fills his song with those beautiful traits of real affection which lovers alone can feel or write. In him there is no covert expression, nor overweening affectation ; nothing of that silky texture of versification, nor of those hereditary classical images and ideas which courtly love has sanctioned. He knows only the language of *nature,* and the imagery of *affection.* He understands little about those *unapproachable* civilities of love ; that chivalrous adoration, and awe-smitten reverence of comportment which are so much cried up by the *gentle* critics, and ladies of excessively polished minds and sickened sensibility. But the " trysted hour " at even ; the endearing and familiar confidence of the short "arm-grips " of love ; mutual promises, sealed by holy kisses : these are the seeds of lovers' poesy, and the heaven which prompts inspiration !

The dancings and revelry at Halloween ; the tryster dancings and singing ; the New-year's-day diversions ; in short, all the " old use and wonts " of their fathers have almost entirely disappeared. They are certainly much better educated than ever ; almost every pupil in the Lowland schools being instructed in English grammar and in the rudiments of the Latin tongue.* But they begin to lose their vigorous originality of character by

---

* Mr. James Gray, of the Edinburgh High School, a man of learning and acute observation, informed me that in the whole course of his life he never met but one Scotchman among the lower classes of society who was ignorant of reading and writing. From this fact, we may partly account for the superiority of the peasantry of Scotland over those of every other country.

attempting to copy the more polished and artificial manners of their neighbours.

So great and rapid, indeed, has been the change, that in a few years the songs and ballads here selected would have been irrecoverably forgotten.

The old cottars (the trysters of other years) are mostly dead in good old age ; and their children are pursuing the bustle of commerce, frequently in foreign climates. The names of their bards have been sought after in vain ; they live only in song, where they have celebrated their social attachments.

It is affecting to think that poets, capable perhaps, of the wild creations of Milton ; the bewitching landscapes and tenderness of Thomson; the faithful nature of Ramsay; or the sublimity, eloquent pathos, and humour of Burns—it is affecting to think that they lie below the turf, and all that can now be redeemed from the oblivious wreck of their genius is a few solitary fragments of song ! But these remnants show the richness of the minds which produced them ; they impress us with a noble idea of peasant abilities, and a sacred reverence for their memory.

Such might have been the fate even of ROBERT BURNS, had not a happy combination of adverse and fortunate circumstances brought his works before the public tribunal. Some stranger might a short while hence, have been gathering up the ruins of his mighty genius, and wondering while he collected them in morsels from the remembrance of tradition; nor need it be deemed extravagant to assert, that Nithsdale and Galloway have at some period of fifty years back, nourished among their harvesting and pastoral vallies, a rustic bard, who sung the loves and feelings of his fellow-peasants, and who bemoaned in undying strains, the deplorable ravages of 1745, and, perhaps, shared in the general and desolating ruin.

With the Revolution commences the era of *Jacobite Song*. The romantic spirit of warrior-adventure had begun to leave the Scotch. It hovered around them like a decaying flame, after the quenching of those deadly feuds which feasted on the richest blood of the sister kingdoms. Those warlike Songs which stirred the valour of their ancestors began to fade along with it. The quarrels of rival houses, and private family-broils had now entirely ceased; and the Caledonian muse was doffing her steely weeds, and piping of rural love, and sweet tranquillity, when the fatal Rebellion of 1715 restored the gory plumes to her cap, and wreathed her brows with laurels dripping in the blood of her country. It was but a momentary glimpse for the poetic exploit of warlike ballad : but among the peasantry it gained a surer hold. They beheld, with a pity prompt on revenge, the fall of many of their most popular nobility. They were secretly attached to their beloved Stuarts. This was the rise of many of their finest Jacobite ballads and songs, which, for bitter humour, and manly feeling, are scarcely surpassed by the compositions of any age or nation.

The rash and disastrous attempt of the brave, the gallant, but unfortunate *Charles*, drew on unhappy Scotland the awful punishment affixed to Rebellion ; a punishment that was inflicted with so unrelenting a hand, that the prophecy of the fanatic *Peden* seemed now fully accomplished—"Scotland ! the time is nigh when we may ride fifty miles 'mang thy hills and thy vallies, nor find a reeking house, nor hear a crawing cock."

This is the second era of Jacobite Song.   Many of the afflicting and plaintive kind belong to this period.   The awful visitations of the *Duke of Cumberland* are yet remembered among the peasantry with horror ! His savage butcheries deeply imprinted themselves into the hearts of the Scotch.   The Songs and fragments which are here gleaned from among the peasantry bear evidence of this ; they want the playful irony which figures in the productions of their predecessors, and seem touched with the heavy hand of sorrow and grief.

It would be superfluous to offer any apology for the political tendency of these Jacobite Ballads.   Time has now softened down those animosities which, at a former period, would have invoked the vigour of the law on those who ventured to sympathize in the fate of the unfortunate Chevalier, or to praise the loyalty of his adherents; and a Briton can now enter into the feelings and attachments of his ancestors without having the rod of prosecution held over him. The rival claims of *Stuart* and *Brunswick* are to the present generation no more a matter of dispute than those of *York* and *Lancaster :* they have been for ever set at rest by the total extinction of the ancient line of the native kings of England. In this, as in all our civil wars, the question of right has been decided by an appeal to arms; and the victorious party has claimed the privilege of branding the vanquished with the stigma of rebellion. It is a wise remark of the patriotic *Fletcher*, that "as the most just and "honourable enterprizes when they fail, are accounted in "the number of rebellions; so all attempts, however "unjust, if they succeed, always purge themselves of all "guilt and suspicion." Posterity, however, are bound to do justice to the character of those men who devoted their lives to what *they* conceived to be the just cause; their fidelity and loyalty have a double claim on our respect, when we consider that they were our ancestors—our countrymen; and that they were denounced as traitors only because they were unsuccessful. It is remarkable, that on the side of Prince *Charles*, all the national poets have ranged themselves, from those who flourished in his day, down to *Burns* and *Campbell*. A romantic enthusiasm, and a warmth of feeling, have occasioned this partiality; and the Editor cannot but avow, that he was prompted by a portion of kindred sentiment, to follow, at an humble distance, in presenting these remains of Scottish loyalty to a liberal and enlightened public.

The Ballads and Songs are gleaned from among the peasantry of *Nithsdale,* and the *skirts* of *Galloway,* adjoining to it. They were never printed before, and are ripe in the sentiments and feelings of their forefathers, and often deliciously mixed with their humour. To those who wish to know how the peasantry think and feel, these *remains* will be acceptable. They may be considered as so many unhewn altars raised to rural love, and local humour and opinion, by the GENIUS of unlettered rusticity.

In works of compilation like the present, the labour of an Editor, however severe, is least apparent, and as far as regards the public, of very inferior consideration. It may be proper, however, to say a few words respecting the remarks which are interspersed through the present volume.

It has been my purpose to avoid the mistake into which collectors are prone to fall, of heaping on their materials a mass of extraneous lumber in the shape of facts and dates, of minute discussions and conjectural emendations, equally perplexing to themselves and to the reader. It is by no means a subject of boast that I have avoided this reproach, for, circumstanced as I was, to have incurred it would have been unpardonable.

In the progress of this collection, it was necessary to have personal intercourse with the peasantry, in whose traditions these Remains were preserved. From a race of men so interesting, and so rich in original character, volumes of curious and valuable remark might be gathered; hence from access to a mine so abundant, it was more a business of selection than of toil, to derive details which might establish what was doubtful, and illustrate what was obscure. At the same time these Remains by exhibiting masterly sketches of the popular genius which produced them, naturally excite a curiosity in readers of every taste, to behold the portrait more fully delineated. Presuming on the excitement of this curiosity, I have ventured to describe, at some length, the domestic manners, the rural occupations, the passions, the attachments, the prejudices, and the superstitions which characterise the peasantry of Nithsdale and Galloway.

These details were in part necessary to make the poetry understood, and if they should have exceeded the bounds which a rigid critic might prescribe, they will not, it is hoped, be considered wholly irrevelant to the purpose I have had in view.

In point of style, they lay no claim to the praise of elegance or refinement; for as they were dictated by strictly local observation, they were written with a sole regard to fidelity and truth. Should the outline be found correct, the colouring vivid, and the whole likeness striking, it is a matter of very little moment that the picture appear unrecommended by the graces of laborious embellishment.

I cannot dismiss this volume without gratefully acknowledging the ready assistance I received while collecting the materials, from all persons to whom my design was communicated; particularly from *Mrs. Copland*, of *Dalbeattie*, in *Galloway*, and her niece *Miss Macartney*, and likewise from *Mr. Allan Cunningham*, of *Dumfries*.

Mrs. Copland's exquisite taste has rescued from oblivion many fine remains of Song; and has illustrated them by remarks equally curious and valuable. On a review of the interesting communications with which she has enriched this collection, the reader will regret that her literary diffidence should have at all restrained her pen in a task which it was so well qualified to perform. It were but justice to acknowledge the benefit which these communications have conferred on the Editor; but his own feelings prompt him to a warmer expression of gratitude for her benevolence in opening to him those hidden treasures of Scottish Song, of which he had been so earnestly in search. To her lovely and amiable niece, Miss Macartney, he would also offer the homage of his thanks as to the Rural Muse of Galloway, who, with a magic hand, had awakened those native strains which were the delight of a simple and pastoral age; and which, in the bustle of commerce, are no longer heard.

To Mr. Allan Cunningham, who, in the humble and laborious profession of a mason, has devoted his leisure hours to the cultivation of a genius naturally of the first order, I cannot sufficiently express my obligations. He entered into my design with the enthusiasm of a poet; and was my guide through the rural haunts of Nithsdale and Galloway; where his variously interesting and animated conversation beguiled the tediousness of the toil; while his local knowledge, his refined taste, and his indefatigable industry, drew from obscurity many pieces which adorn this collection, and which, without his aid, would have eluded my research.

To those of his own countrymen who disrelish every thing that is of Scottish growth, merely because they do not understand, or are not accustomed to it, the Editor foresees that these *Native Songsters* will not be very welcome. Even one of the first among living English poets once observed to him, in a conversation respecting BURNS, that "he was a *clever fellow;* but it was a pity he wrote in such a *strange, outlandish* dialect!"

To this sort of prejudiced people an argument will not avail; and, perhaps, the following little story may be thrown away upon them.

"A country gentleman from the west of Scotland, being occasionally in England for a few weeks, was, one delightful summer evening, asked to hear the nightingale; his friend informing him at the same time, that this bird was a *native of England*, and never to be heard in his own country.   After he had listened with attention, for some time, upon being asked, if he was not much de-lighted with the nightingale, "It's a' very gude," replied he, "it's a' very gude ; but I wadna gie *the wheeple of a whaup* for a' the nightingales that ever sang."

R. H. C.

London,
July, 1810.

SONGS

OF

THE NITHSDALE AND GALLOWAY PEASANTRY.

CLASS I.—SENTIMENTAL.

THERE is a noble sublimity, a heart-melting tenderness, in some of our ancient ballads, which shew them to be the work of a masterly hand: and it has often given me many a heart-ache to reflect, that such glorious old bards—bards, who very probably owed all their talents to native genius, yet have described the exploits of heroes, the pangs of disappointment, and the meltings of love, with such fine strokes of nature—that their very names (O how mortifying to a bard's vanity!) are now "buried among the wreck of things which were."

BURNS.

THE LORD'S MARIE.

THE Editor is indebted to Mrs. Copland of Dalbeattie, in Galloway, for this song, and for the following notices and remarks respecting it.

" This old song is founded on a traditional story of a daughter of Lord Maxwell, of Nithsdale, accompanying, in disguise, a peasant to a rustic dancing tryste. 'The lord's daughter sae gay,' was discovered through the disguise of her rustic habiliments. Tradition places the song at the Revolution, 1688. The language is more modern, but the ideas belong to that period.

' The Lord's Marie ' is one of those songs which keep a lasting hold of the mind by their enticing tale, and simple dramatic narration. The first verse is very characteristic and natural. It is told with all the native dignity of affection which belongs to an unlettered rustic, unshackled by the harnessing of refinement. In the second and third verses we are lifted at once into the dancing tryste.

Her lover's silence, and her supping the 'bluid-red wine,' are happily imagined and executed. There is a tradition extant, that Lord Cassilis' lady, who eloped with Johnnie Faa, the gypsie laddie, had so delicate and pure a skin, that the red wine could be seen through it while she was drinking.

In the fourth verse, the arch fiddler is drawn with real humour, and gives a pleasant turn to the ballad.

The fifth verse is touched with all the energy of love; and yet with so delicate a hand, that the holiness of the female mind must feel its meek and staid composure delighted and edified with so sweet a delineation.

> 'And, O! her hinney breath lift her locks,
> As through the dance she flew,'

Is an elegant and naïvé stroke not easily paralleled. In the sixth verse, where her gold-embroidered garter and broach discover her rank, there is a tenderness and feeling mingled with the lovely confusion of maiden innocence and affection, which will be strongly felt by every reader of taste and goodness. The last verse is strongly impressed with the Scottish character. It is a beautiful example of that engaging confidence which purity and innocence can bring from the heart.

The artless and undisguised expression touches the heart more than all the courtly magnificence which some of your 'Falkland-bred,' glove-handed bards, have larded their verses with.

The song is rendered more interesting by being given as the recital of the peasant. It will survive amid the wreck of those songs which society tramples down in its progress."

THE LORD'S MARIE.

I.

THE Lord's Marie has kepp'd her locks
    Up wi' a gowden kame,
An' she has put on her net-silk hose,
    An' awa to the tryste* has gane.
O saft, saft fell the dew on her locks,
    An' saft, saft on her brow ;
Ae sweet drap fell on her strawberrie lip,
    An' I kiss'd it aff I trow !

II.

"O whare gat ye that leal maiden,
    Sae jimpy laced an' sma' ?
O whare gat ye that young damsel,
    Wha dings our lasses a' ?
"O whare gat ye that bonnie, bonnie lass,
    Wi' Heaven in her ee ?
O here's ae drap o' the damask wine ;—
    Sweet maiden, will ye pree ?†

III.

Fu' white, white was her bonnie neck,
    Twist wi' the satin twine,
But ruddie, ruddie grew her hawse,‡
    While she supp'd the bluid-red wine.

---

* *Tryste*, a place of meeting.
† *To pree*, to taste.   ‡ *Hawse*, the throat.

"Come, here's thy health, young stranger doo,*
    Wha wears the gowden kame ;—
This night will mony drink thy health,
    An ken na wha to name.

IV.

Play me up "Sweet Marie," I cry'd,
    An' loud the piper blew,—
But the fiddler play'd ay *Struntum strum*,
    An' down his bow he threw.
"Here's thy kin' health i' the ruddie red wine,
    Fair dame o' the stranger land !
For never a pair o' een before
    Could mar my gude bow-hand.

V.

Her lips were a cloven hinney-cherrie,
    Sae tempting to the sight ;
Her locks owre alabaster brows,
    Fell like the morning light.
An' O ! her hinney breath lift her locks,
    As through the dance she flew,
While luve laugh'd in her bonnie blue ee,
    An' dwalt on her comely mou'.

VI.

"Loose hings yere broider'd gowd garter,
    Fair ladie, dare I speak ?"

---

* *Doo*, dove.

She, trembling, lift her silky hand
  To her red, red flushing cheek.
" Ye've drapp'd, ye've drapp'd yere broach o' gowd,
  Thou Lord's daughter sae gay,"
The tears o'erbrimm'd her bonnie blue ee,
  "O come, O come away !"—

VII.

" O maid, unbar the siller belt,*
  To my chamber let me win,
An' tak this kiss, thou peasant youth,
  I daur na let ye in.
An' tak', quo' she, this kame o' gowd,
  Wi' my lock o' yellow hair,
For meikle my heart forebodes to me,
  I never maun meet ye mair !"

---

* *Belt*, bolt.

BONNIE LADY ANN.

(From the Recitation of Miss CATHERINE MACARTNEY, of Hacket Leaths, Galloway.)

A fairer specimen of romantic Scottish love than is contained in this song, is rarely to be met with. It was first introduced to Nithsdale and Galloway about thirty years ago, by a lady whose mind was deranged. She wandered from place to place, followed by some tamed sheep. The old people describe her as an amiable and mild creature. She would lie all night under the shade of some particular tree, with her sheep around her. They were as the ewe-lamb in the scripture parable;— they lay in her bosom, ate of her bread, drank of her cup, and were unto her as daughters. Thus she wandered through part of England, and the low part of Scotland; esteemed, respected, pitied, and wept for by all! She was wont to sing this song unmoved, until she came to the last verse, and then she burst into tears. The old tree, under which she sat with her sheep, is now cut down. The schoolboys always paid a kind of religious respect to it. It never was the " dools," nor the " butt ;" nor were the " outs and ins," nor the hard-fought game of " England and Scotland,"* ever played about it :

---

* A description of these games will be found in the Appendix (A.)

but there, on fine Sabbath evenings, the old women sat down and read their Bibles; the young men and maidens learned their Psalms, and then went home full of the meek and holy composure of religion.

BONNIE LADY ANN.

I.

THERE's kames o' hinney 'tween my luve's lips,
  An' gowd amang her hair,
Her breasts are lapt in a holie veil,
  Nae mortal een keek* there.
What lips dare kiss, or what hand dare touch,
  Or what arm o' luve dare span
The hinney lips, the creamy loof,
  Or the waist o' Lady Ann !

II.

She kisses the lips o' her bonnie red rose,
  Wat wi' the blobs o' dew ;
But nae gentle lip, nor simple lip,
  Maun touch her Ladie mou.
But a broider'd belt wi' a buckle o' gowd,
  Her jimpy† waist maun span,
O she's an armfu' fit for heaven,
  My bonnie Lady Ann !

III.

Her bower casement is latticed wi' flowers,
  Tied up wi' silver thread,
An' comely sits she in the midst,
  Men's longing een to feed.

---

* *To keek*, to peep, to take a stolen glance.
† *Jimpy*, slender.

She waves the ringlets frae her cheek,
  Wi' her milky, milky han',
An' her cheeks seem touch'd wi' the finger o' God,
  My bonnie Lady Ann !

IV.

The morning cloud is tassel'd wi' gowd,
  Like my luve's broider'd cap,
An' on the mantle which my love wears
  Are monie a gowden drap.
Her bonnie eebree's a holie arch
  Cast by no earthlie han',
An' the breath o' God's atween the lips
  O' my bonnie Lady Ann !

V.

I am her father's gardener lad,
  An' poor, poor is my fa' ;*
My auld mither gets my wee, wee fee,
  Wi' fatherless bairnies twa :
My Ladie comes, my Ladie gaes
  Wi' a fou and kindly han',
O the blessing o' God maun mix wi' my luve,
  An' fa' on' Lady Ann !

There is a variation in the last verse well worth preserving. Indeed, a deal of unseemly chaff had inter-

------

* *Fa'*, lot, fate.

mixed with the heavy grain, which has cost a little win-
nowing and sieving.

> " I am her daddie's gardener lad,
>   An' poor, poor is my fa';
> My auld mither gets my sair-won fee,
>   Wi' fatherless bairns twa.
> My een are bauld, they dwall on a place,
>   Where I darena mint my han',
> But I water, and tend, and kiss the flowers
>   O' my bonnie Lady Ann."*

---

* These verses were accompanied by the following remarks, addressed to the
Editor, by his friend Allan Cunningham, of Dumfries.

"You will be pleased to note down this old song to the muse of Nithsdale and
Galloway. She is a gude, sonsie, sweet an' kindlie quean; and tho' she may
gang a wee thing "high kilted" at times, she's gawcie an' modest for a' that,
an' winna disgrace your southern gudeness."

SHE'S GANE TO DWALL IN HEAVEN.

(NITHSDALE.)

Historical notices on these songs are the most difficult things to be procured imaginable.   They are below the dignity of the historian, and tradition has so fabled them that we dare scarcely trust her report.   We may justly say they are like wild-flower seeds scattered by the winds of heaven.   Who can tell the mother which gathered them, or the wind which sowed them?   They rise up only to flourish unseen, or to be trodden down and to wither.

This ballad is said to be written about the time of the Reformation, on a daughter of the Laird Maxwell, of Cowhill, on the banks of the Nith, called by the peasantry, "The Lilie of Nithsdale."   "She faded in her place," at the age of nineteen.

SHE'S gane to dwall in heaven, my lassie,
   She' gane to dwall in heaven :
Ye're owre pure, quo' the voice o' God,
   For dwalling out o' heaven !

O what'll she do in heaven, my lassie ?
   O what'll she do in heaven ?
She'll mix her ain thoughts wi' angels' sangs,
   An' make them mair meet for heaven.

She was beloved by a', my lassie,
   She was beloved by a' ;
But an angel fell in luve wi' her,
   An' took her frae us a'.

Low there thou lies my lassie,
   Low there thou lies ;
A bonnier form ne'er went to the yird,*
   Nor frae it will arise !

Fu' soon I'll follow thee, my lassie,
   Fu' soon I'll follow thee ;
Thou left me nought to covet ahin',
   But took gudeness sel' wi' thee.

I looked on thy death-cold face, my lassie,
   I looked on thy death-cold face ;
Thou seemed a lilie new cut i' the bud,
   An' fading in its place.

---

* Earth.

I looked on thy death-shut eye, my lassie,
   I looked on thy death-shut eye ;
An' a lovelier light in the brow of heaven
   Fell time shall ne'er destroy.

Thy lips were ruddie and calm, my lassie,
   Thy lips were ruddie and calm ;
But gane was the holie breath o' heaven
   To sing the evening Psalm.

There's naught but dust now mine, lassie,
   There's naught but dust now mine ;
My saul's wi' thee i' the cauld grave,
   An' why should I stay behin' !

———

This ballad was copied from the recitation of a young country-girl. She observed that it was a great favourite of her mother's, but seldom sung, as its open familiarity with God made it too daring for Presbyterian strictness. These elegiac verses, though in some instances they pass the bounds of the simple and natural pathetic, express strongly the mingled feelings of grief and devotion which follow the loss of some beloved object. There are degrees of affliction corresponding with the degrees of our attachment and regard, and surely the most tender of attachments must be deplored by affliction the most poignant. This may account for, and excuse those expressions in this song, which border on extravagance ; but it must be confessed that the first stanza, with every allowance, is reprehensible from its open and daring

confidence in the Deity.   The rest are written in a strain
of solemn and feeling eloquence which must find an
echo in every bosom.   The effusion is somewhat too
serious for a song ; it has all the holiness of a psalm, and
would suffer profanation by being set to a common tune.

THOU HAST SWORN BY THY GOD, MY JEANIE.

(GALLOWAY AND NITHSDALE.)

These verses are copied from the recitation of a worthy old man, now "raked i' the mools," as the Scotch phrase is.   With him have perished many beautiful songs, remnants of the times which were.   He was a dissenter from the Church of Scotland, and had all that stern severity of demeanour, and rigidness of mind, which belong to those trained in the old school of divinity, under the iron discipline of Scottish Presbyterianism. Yet when kept aloof from religious dispute, when his native goodness was not touched with the sour leaven of bigotry, he was a man, as we may truly say with scripture, "after God's own heart."   There is a characteristic trait of him which will lighten the darkness of superstition which gave it birth.   In that violent persecution* in the reigns of James the Seventh, and the second Charles, one of the persecuted preachers took refuge among the wild hills behind Kirkmahoe, in the county of Dumfries. On a beautiful green-topped hill, called the *Wardlaw*,

---

* See the Appendix (B.)

C

was raised a pulpit of sods, where he preached to his congregation. General Dalzell hastened on with his dragoons, and dispersed the assembly. This consecrated the spot. Our worthy old patriarch, in the fine Sabbath evenings, would go with his wife and children to the *Wardlaw,* though some miles of rough road distant,— seat himself in the preacher's place, and *"take the Beuk,"** with his family around him. He kneeled down, and with all the flow of religious eloquence, held converse with his God. This song was his favourite, and he usually sung it at Halloweens, at kirk-suppers, and other trystes.

---

* See the Appendix (C.)

THOU HAST SWORN BY THY GOD, MY JEANIE.

I.

THOU hast sworn by thy God, my Jeanie,
    By that pretty white hand o' thine,
And by a' the lowing stars in heaven,
    That thou wad ay be mine !
And I hae sworn by my God, my Jeanie,
    And by that kind heart o' thine,
By a' the stars sown thick owre heaven,
    That thou shalt ay be mine !

II.

Then foul fa' the hands that wad loose sic bands,
    An' the heart that wad part sic love ;
But there's nae hand can loose my band,
    But the finger o' God above.
Tho' the wee, wee cot maun be my bield,
    An' my claithing e'er sae mean,
I wad lap me up rich i' the faulds o' luve,
    Heaven's armfu' o' my Jean !

III.

Her white arm wad be a pillow for me,
    Fu' safter than the down,
An' luve wad winnow owre us his kind, kind, wings
    An' sweetly I'd sleep an' soun'.

Come here to me, thou lass o' my luve,
   Come here and kneel wi' me,
The morn is fu' o' the presence o' my God,
   An' I canna pray but* thee.

IV.

The morn-wind is sweet 'mang the beds o' new
     flowers,
   The wee birds sing kindlie an' hie,
Our gude-man leans owre his kale-yard dyke,
   An' a blythe auld bodie is he.
The *Beuk* maun be taen whan the carle comes
     hame,
   Wi' the holie psalmodie,
And thou maun speak o' me to thy God,
   And I will speak o' thee !

   This exquisite mixture of love and reverence to God is hardly paralleled in the annals of song.   It is warmly touched with the holy breath of love, and yet may well beseem the devotional lips of the good old man who did it honour by singing it.   It seems to have been written in those fluctuating times, when the hands which were *taking the Beuk* would have been reeking with blood— when the field of deadly strife became in a few minutes the consecrated ground of religious devotion.   In those

---

* *But,* without.

times love was tempered with religion ; books were composed in support of this extraordinary union.   This song is a fine example of devotion, chastening the passion of love so as not to extinguish but to refine it to a purer flame.   When the turbulence of war had subsided, there was time for appreciating the blessings of repose, and for composing songs glowing with rural imagery, and ripe with rural sentiment.

To these times this song evidently belongs.   Men then talked openly of conversing with God, and of wrestling with him in prayer.

> "An' thou maun speak o' me to thy God,
> An' I will speak o' thee."*

---

* These sentiments proceed from that strong and daring familiarity which enthusiasm inspires, and which conscious worth dictates. In the life of *Alexander Peden* a prayer is preserved which affords a singular illustration of this remark. This prayer was made after the last sermon he preached, in which he thus addresses the Deity : "Lord, thou hast been both good and kind to old *Sanny*, through a long tract of time, and given him many years in thy service, which has been but as so many months : but now he is tired of thy world, and hath done all the good in it that he will do, let him awa with the honesty that he has, for he will gather no more."

Alexander Peden is the patriarch of the Cameronian sect. His prophecies were gleaned about the year 1720, from the voice of tradition, and interwoven with his Memoirs by one of his enthusiastic disciples, who believed he saw his denunciations faithfully fulfilling. They are written with great earnestness and simplicity. The volume was long a school-book in the private seminaries of. Cameronian discipline.

Peden was of a character admirably adapted to meet the exigencies of the persecuting times in which he lived. He had great personal courage, accompanied with an astonishing promptitude of mind. A firm believer in those powerful visions of futurity which a vivid imagination presented to him, be was stern and severe in his manners ; hence his rebukes bad the air of denunciation, and his "depart from me, ye cursed" was delivered not in the savage anathematizing tone of a Romish prelate, but with the calm dignity of a being impressed with the belief of an exalted and immediate intercourse with the Deity himself.

His invitation of the maiden to come and kneel beside
him is natively characteristic :

> " The morn is fu' o' the presence o' my God,
> An' I canna pray *but* thee."

There is a fragment of an old ballad which will
exemplify, in a beautiful but affecting manner, those
religious and amorous mixtures of which we have been
speaking.

It is given from the recitation of Miss CATHERINE
MACARTNEY.

LADIE JEAN'S LUVE.

A FRAGMENT.

*   *   *   *

Bluidie was the braid saddle lap,
  An' bluidie was the crupper,
An' bluidie were my true luve's hands
  As we sat down to supper.

There's water i' the siller dish,
  Gae wash thae hands sae bluidie :
But my luve washed i' the water clear,
  An' never made it ruddie.

An' he took up the snawie claith,
  Which my twa hands did border,
He rubbed ay on his bluidie hands,
  An' never made it redder.

An' ay he dighted his wat, wat cheek,
  While the holie beuk was bringing,
An' ay he looked on his bluidie hands,
  While the Psalm was singing.

An' "*Let us pray*," quo' the gude auld carle,
  An' "Let us pray," quo' he ;
But my love sat on the lang-settle,
  An' never a knee bent he.

"*Kneel down, kneel down*," quo' the gude old carle,
  "*Kneel down*, an' pray wi' me—"
O there's mercy wi' God for thee, auld carle,
  But there's nae mercy for me.

     *   *   *   *

Familiar simplicity, pourtraying the emotions of the heart, in those fine traits which so strongly express the peculiar feelings and tints of character belonging to their period of composition, is the marked feature of Scottish Song. An ingenious antiquary might collect from these ballads and songs, could their dates be ascertained, the local history of feeling and ideas, which shoot forth in the progress of society. These are peculiar to certain districts of country. The following verse may be adduced as fitting the Lowlands, where the severe sense of deep religion is strikingly visible in every old person. It is a pious address of a mother to a daughter, concerning her lover.

He disna tak the Beuk :
Een's the mair pitie !

He says nae grace to his meat,
   An' graceless maun he be :
Whan he's nae gratefu' to his God,
   He canna be guid to thee.

A noble sentiment, which ought to be written in letters
of gold !

There is another stray verse, which, though told with
a little more sprightliness, is cast in the same mint of
opinion with the preceding.

My lad canna kneel at the Beuk
   For fyling the knees o' his breeks,
His cheeks are tosie* and dry,
   Whan tears are on a' our cheeks.
He downa sing at the Psalm
   For spoiling his mim, mim mou :
The lips which sing na to God,
   Should never a maiden woo.

There are now perhaps few maidens who would refuse
a husband for these psalm-singing failings.

Specimens might be multiplied by an assiduous collector :—

His lips are nae psalm-lips,
   Tent what I'm saying ;
Fu' o' sang-profanity,
   Ken nought o' praying :

---

* *Tosie*, a cheerful glow on the countenance.

Sae trimlie he fits the reel
  Wi' ilka gawkie,
He'll dance wi' ye, "O'er Bogie,"*
  Maiden, and wrack ye.

The Deil's legs bore him
  I' the road o' grace ance,
Whan he set weel the sacking-gown,
  I' the stool o' Repentance.†
      *   *   *   *

Dancing was and is yet counted a heinous sin with some of those sects, overstrait-laced in Calvinism.

Sermons were composed on the immodesty of demeanour and loose ideas engendered by dancing. Some tolerated it in this extraordinary way. "The lads and lasses must dance with their backs to one another, for the warm intermixture of breath smells too rank of fornication."‡

---

* Alluding to an old song, of which nothing remains but the chorus.
    "1 will awa wi' my love,
    1 will awa wi' her,
    Tho' a' my kin had sworn and said
    I'll *o'er Bogie* wi' her."

† A description of this vile stool will be found in the Appendix (D).

‡ "The most innocent amusements and the most profligate dissipation were alike proscribed. Cards and *dancing* were interdicted as snares of Satan, dangerous, or at least unsuitable to the people of God. The feasts and domestic pastimes appropriated to the winter-solstice, the revels and public diversions of the people, even the Christmas recess of the Courts of Law, were suppressed as superstitious; the sports of the field were forbidden to the clergy; nor durst the most popular amongst them indulge in the most innocent recreations, without a dispensation from the Presbytery for the preservation of their health."
                        LAING'S HIST. OF SCOTLAND, iii. 430.

D

The last fragment seems to be a satire on religious advices in the choice of lovers.   It is put into the mouth of one of those *feerie auld wives* who can walk upon the very edge of delicacy in their advice, and counsel in the real spirit of broad humour.

That these songs are mostly forgotten, or only remembered in fragments, must be attributed to the features of Calvinism softening from their strictness into the milder glow of affection and good-will.

THE BROKEN HEART OF ANNIE.

HERE's a dud to hap its head,
An' a clout to rowe* the feetie o't,—
Here's twa arms can nurse it weel,
Twa een can greet wi' pity o't.
But whare's my mither a' the while?
She'll hear the wee, wee greetie o't.

O lie thee still, my sweet, wee babe,
Lift nae thy white wee hannie, O ;
Thou art thy father frae the chin to the ee,
But sae fause as him thou cannie, O.
O, if thou pruive as fause as him
Thou hast nae't frae thy mammie, O.
* * * * * *

Its nae thy gowd, nor thy siller clear,
Nor thy laced caps sae bonnie, O—
Can gie me back that peace I tint,
Or heal the heart of Annie O !—
But speak to thy God of the vows ye broke,
For ye hae broken monie, O.†

---

* *To rowe*, to roll.

† This faithful picture of the feelings of a smitten heart has an affecting

parallel in a female's address to her infant, printed in a work called the *Northern Lass*, or the *Nest of Fools*, 1606.

> Peace, wayward Bairn : o cease thy mone,
> Thy far more wayward daddy's gone,
> And never will recalled be,
> By cries of either thee or me :—
>   For should we cry,
>   Until we die,
> We could not scant his cruelty.
>   Ballow, Ballow, &c.

> He needs might in himself foresee,
> What thou successively might'st be ;
> And could he then, though me forego,
> His infant leave, ere he did know
>   How like the dad
>   Would be the lad
> In time to make fond maidens glad,
>   Ballow, Ballow, &c.

HABBIE'S FRAE HAME.

(GALLOWAY.)

By the side o' yon cleugh,* whare the burnie rins shill,
    A lassie sat sighing and spinning her lane ;
" O, gin the waes o' my heart wad lie still ;——
    There'll never be peace till our Habbie comes
        hame.

" As my wheel gaes round, my lint I spread,
    Lint that I mean for bibs to my bairn ;
The warp shall be blue, and the waft shall be red,
    An' how braw we'll be a' whan our Habbie comes
        hame.

" That morning he left us our cock never crew,
    Our gray clocking hen she gaed keckling her lane ;
The Gowk frae the craft never cried ' cuckoo !'
    That wearifu' morning our Habbie left hame.

" Whan the wind blaws loud and tirls our strae,
    An' a' our house-sides are dreeping wi' rain,
An' ilka burn rows frae the bank to the brae,
    I weep for our Habbie wha rows i' the main.

" Whan the wars are owre, an' quiet is the sea,
    On board the Culloden our Hab will come hame ;
My slumbers will then be as sweet as the Dee,
    An' how blythe we'll be a' whan our Habbie comes
        hame."

---

* *Cleugh*, the cleft of a hill, a woody recess.

THE RETURN OF SPRING.

(GALLOWAY.)

I.

CAULD winter is awa, my luve,
And spring is in her prime,
The breath o' God stirs a' to life,
The grasshoppers to chime:
The birds canna contain themsels
Upon the sprouting tree,
But loudlie, loudlie, sing o' luve,
A theme which pleaseth me.

II.

The blackbird is a pawkie loun,
An' kens the gate o' luve;
Fu' well the sleekit mavis kens
The melting lilt maun muve.
The gowdspink woos in gentle note,
And ever singeth he,
"Come here, come here, my spousal dame,"
A theme which pleaseth me.

III.

What says the sangster Rose-linnet?
His breast is beating high,
"Come here, come here, my ruddie mate,
The gate o' luve to try."

The lav'roc calls his freckled mate,
　　Frae near the sun's ee-bree,
" Come make on the knowe our nest of luve,"
　　A theme which pleaseth me.

IV.

The hares hae brought forth twins, my luve,
　　Sae has the cushat doo ;*
The raven croaks a safter way,
　　His sootie luve to woo:
And nought but luve, luve breathes around,
　　Frae hedge, frae field, an' tree,
Soft whispering luve to Jeanie's heart,
　　A theme which pleaseth me.

V.

O Lassie, is thy heart mair hard
　　Than mavis frae the bough ;
Say maun the hale creation wed,
　　And Jean remain to woo?
Say has the holie lowe o' luve
　　Ne'er lighten'd in your ee?
O, if thou canst na feel for pain,
　　Thou art nae theme for me !

　　This song was procured from the young girl who preserved the stanzas beginning " She's gane to dwall in Heaven." Her remarks are strikingly correct.

---

* *Cushat doo*, the stockdove.

"This sweet and spirited song contains an amiable portrait of a fine and virtuous mind. The birds are all of the soft and tender kind, and we even think we hear their melody. The timidity of the hare is a happy emblem of the retiring shyness of the female character. The wood-pigeons, and the raven, softening his uncouthness at the voice of love, are happy, and well imagined. The opening of the song presents a beautiful picture of spring —the breath of God stirring the whole creation to life— that warm and renovating influence of spring—'the birds canna contain themscls,' is pregnant with love. It is, on the whole, a pretty example of Scottish pastoral.

"It used to be sung at haymakings by young lads : and the girls repeated the last line of the verses along with them. There is an old song which I heard my aunt singing, that appears to me spirited and natural."

My lassie's come to our town,
    To our town to dwall a wee,
An', haith ! wi' me she's kindlie grown,
    Her twa blue een they tell me sae.
Kind luve's 'neath her ee-bree,
    And aft I court it (Gude forgie me !)
I' the kirk whare nane but God can see me ;
    But lover's looks maun halie be.

What like may your lassie be,
    The lassie wham ye lo'e sae weel ?

Kin' luve's in mony an ee,
  For gleg's* the glance which lovers steal.
At the kirk look for the fairest,
  At the dance look out the rarest,
An' haith ! in short love-grips the dearest,
  Her kissing lips ay tell me sae.

---

* *Gleg*, quick.

THE LOVELY LASS OF PRESTON MILL.

I.

THE lark had left the evening cloud,
    The dew fell saft, the wind was lowne,
Its gentle breath amang the flowers
    Scarce stirred the thistle's tap o' down ;
The dappled swallow left the pool,
    The stars were blinking owre the hill,
As I met amang the hawthorns green,
    The lovely lass of Preston Mill.

II.

Her naked feet amang the grass,
    Seemed like twa dew-gemmed lilies fair ;
Her brows shone comely 'mang her locks,
    Black curling owre her shouthers bare :
Her cheeks were rich wi' bloomy youth ;
    Her lips were like a honey well,
An' heaven seemed looking through her een,
    The lovely lass of Preston Mill.

III.

Quo' I, "fair lass, will ye gang wi' me,
    Whare black cocks craw, and plovers cry?
Sax hills are wooly wi' my sheep,
    Sax vales are lowing wi' my kye :

I hae looked lang for a weel-faur'd lass,
  By Nithsdale's howmes an' monie a hill;"—
She hung her head like a dew-bent rose,
  The lovely lass of Preston Mill.

IV.

Quo' I, " sweet maiden, look nae down,
  But gie's a kiss, and gae wi' me : "
A lovelier face, O ! never looked up,
  And the tears were drapping frae her ee :
' I hae a lad, wha's far awa,
  That weel could win a woman's will;
My heart's already fu' o' love,'
  Quo' the lovely lass of Preston Mill.

V.

" O wha is he wha could leave sic a lass,
  To seek for love in a far countrie ? "—
Her tears drapped down like simmer dew,
  I fain wad hae kissed them frae her ee.
I took but ane o' her comelie cheek;
  " For pity's sake, kind Sir, be still !
My heart is fu' o' ither love,"
  Quo' the lovely lass of Preston Mill.

VI.

She streeked to heaven her twa white hands,
  And lifted up her wat'ry ee ;
"Sae lang's my heart kens ought o' God,
  Or light is gladsome to my ee ;—

While woods grow green, and burns rin clear,
    Till my last drap o' blood be still,
My heart sall haud nae ither love,"
    Quo' the lovely lass of Preston Mill.

VII.

There's comelie maids on Dee's wild banks,
    And Nith's romantic vale is fu' ;
By lanely 'Clouden's hermit stream,
    Dwalls monie a gentle dame, I trow !
O, they are lights of a bonnie kind,
    As ever shone on vale or hill ;
But there's a light puts them a' out,
    The lovely lass of Preston Mill.

FRAGMENT.

(Recovered by Miss C. MACARTNEY.)

GANE were but the winter-cauld,*
And gane were but the snaw,
I could sleep in the wild woods,
Whare primroses blaw.

Cauld's the snaw at my head,
And cauld at my feet,
And the finger o' death at my een,
Closing them to sleep.

Let nane tell my father,
Or my mither sae dear,
I'll meet them baith in heaven,
At the spring o' the year.

The Editor was struck with the resemblance of the following lines to the latter stanzas of the above fragment. He heard them sung to a child by an elderly gentleman, who had learnt them, when a boy, in Yorkshire. From the similiarity of the sentiment, he is inclined to suppose that they descended from one common source, or that the one is an imitation of the other. To

---

* *i. e.* If the winter-cold were but gone.

which of them the merit of originality belongs may be
doubtful ; they are both exquisite ; but there is a touch
of pathos in these lines which goes directly to the heart,
and leaves a sentiment of pity there, which the other
piece fails immediately to excite.

> Make me a grave in yon channel sae deep,
> Lay a stone at my head, and another at my feet;
> That there I may lie and take a lang sleep,
> And adieu to my fause luve for ever !

A philosophic historian has somewhere observed, that
the pathetic consists in the detail of minute circumstances. The above fragment justifies the remark ; and
if the entire song could be recovered, it would doubtless
afford an ampler illustration of it. Indeed, the most
popular of our rustic ballads, when analysed, are found
to consist of common-place figures, and homely sentiments, conveyed in the plainest language ; yet, taken as
a whole, they affect us more powerfully than the elaborate
and polished effusions of what may be called the classic
school of poetry. The simple and wildly pleasing melodies which accompany them, are perfectly characteristic,
and equally surpass in effect the more scientific strains
of modern music. In listening to a rustic ballad we in-
quire not why we are pleased ; it seizes our attention and
captivates our mind like a tale of enchantment, where
" more is meant than meets the ear." Probably its antiquity tends to heighten the charm ; we yield more willingly to the illusion when we consider that we are listening to the same strains which delighted our forefathers,
and which depict the manners of the good old times.

Attempts have lately been made to revive this primitive style of poetry, but they have uniformly proved abortive; and however closely they imitated the ancient model, they were rejected, because they were imitations. Perhaps a further cause of the failure arose from the difficulty of preserving the quaint simplicity of the original without descending into puerility and nonsense; or rather because the simplicity of the original is natural, and that of the imitation affected. Of all men of cultivated genius, Sterne has most successfully drawn from the true source of the pathetic; his most moving scenes are often mere details of the common occurrences of life, and he has contrived from the most trifling incidents to awaken our tenderest sensibilities. But what in him is the result of art, very artfully concealed, is in the unknown authors of our rustic ballads the genuine prompting of uneducated nature. They knew nothing of the philosophy of the mind; they had no choice of the various modes of eloquence by which the heart may be moved; but they followed an unerring rule;—they wrote from the free impulse of their feelings, and they found a response in every bosom. The voice of tradition has confirmed their appeal to the heart, and the applause of posterity has proved, that in a rude age, when the light of reason is uncertain and doubtful, instinct may be a safe and faithful guide. The rustic ballads of our ancestors are still the delight of every age, and of every rank in life; and in general those persons who are most eminent for genius and taste are most enthusiastically charmed with them. As a splendid instance of this truth, we may mention Shakspeare, who has enriched many of his most pathetic scenes with fragments of

ancient song; as in the tender grief of the wronged
Desdemona, or the melancholy of the distracted *Ophelia.*
On some occasions he has introduced them with a
characteristic remark, as in his comedy of "Twelfth Night,"
where the *Duke,* a man of taste and refinement, calls for
the repetition of a song which he had before heard, and
which deeply affected him by its unadorned simplicity,
and rustic pathos.

> " It is silly sooth,
> And dallies wth the innocence of love
> Like the old age."

Come away, come away, death,
And in sad cypress let me be laid ;
  Fly away, fly away, breath ;
I am slain by a fair cruel maid.
My shroud of white, stuck all with yew,
      O, prepare it ;
My part of death no one so true
      Did share it.

Not a flower, not a flower sweet,
On my black coffin let there be strown ;
  Not a friend, not a friend greet
My poor corpse, where my bones shall be thrown.
A thousand thousand sighs to save,
      Lay me, O, where
Sad true lover ne'er find my grave,
      To weep there.

THE AULD CARLE'S WELCOME.

The poetic merit of this song is considerably enhanced from the circumstance of its being founded on a peculiar custom which still prevails in the Lowlands of Scotland.

"To wauke the auld year into the new," is a popular and expressive phrase for watching until twelve o'clock announces the new year, when people are ready at their neighbours' houses with *het-pints*, and buttered cakes, eagerly waiting to be *first-foot*, as it is termed, and to regale the family yet in bed. Much care is taken that the persons who enter be what are called *sonsie folk*, for on the admission of the first-foot depends the prosperity or trouble of the year.

The Gudeman's "Welcome" to his Neighbour Gudewife, here given, is an excellent picture of fire-side felicity, and the old Scottish cast of character. The remembered frolics of their youthful days, and their heavenward look of hereafter, present a truly patriarchal and interesting scene.

———

I.

How's a' wi' my auld Dame,
—My sonsie Dame, my mensfu' dame ;
How's a' the folk at hame,
  Wi' the canty auld Gudeman, Jo ?

F

Sit down in peace my winsome dow,*
Tho' thin thy locks and beld† thy brow,
Thou ance were armfu' fit I trow,
   To mense a kintra en', Jo.—

II.

Ance on a day, in tryster time,
Whan in thy ee love blinkit prime,
And through our teens we bore the gree
   In ilka kintra ha', Jo ;
The lasses gloom'd whan thou did sing,
The lads leaned roun' thee in a ring,
While blythly I took up the spring,
   And bore the mense awa, Jo !

III.

An' haith ! at Kirns‡ we're canty yet,
Amang our bairnses bonnie bairns ;
At brydal shaw, or new house heat,
   We thraw auld age awa, Jo ;
Tho' past the younkers' trysting prime,
Our pows tho' strewed wi' winter's rime,
We've linkit thro' a blythsome time,—
   The gowden age awa, Jo !

IV.

A mirthfu' thing it is an blythe,
To think on't yet, to think on't yet,

---

*Dow, dove.   †Beld, bald.
‡ Kirns, the feast of harvest-home.

Tho' creeping to the grave belyve,
  We're lifted wi' the thought, Jo !
We've fouchten teuch, an' warstled sair,
Out thro' this warl' o' din an' care,
An', haith ! we've something mair than prayer
  To help a poor bodie, Jo !

v.

Reach me the Beuk, my winsome Jean,
My specks bring, and the bairns send in,
I'll wale a kind an' halie thing,
  Seems written just for thee, Jo !
" *The gude auld folk God winna lea !*
Nor thraw their bairns on the wide kintrie ; "*
Then blink fu' blythe, wi' uplift ee,
  Sin' God has taen our han', Jo !

---

* "I have been young, and now am old, yet have I not seen the righteous forsaken, nor his seed begging bread."—PSALM xxxvii. 25.

A WEARY BODIE'S BLYTHE WHAN THE SUN GANGS DOWN.

A WEARY bodie's blythe whan the sun gangs down,
A weary bodie's blythe whan the sun gangs down :
To smile wi' his wife, and to daute wi' his weans,
Wha wadna be blythe whan the sun gangs down.

The simmer sun's lang, an' we're a' toiled sair,
Frae sun-rise to sun-set's a dreigh tack o' care ;
But at hame for to daute 'mang our wee bits o' weans,
We think on our toils an' our cares nae mair.

The Saturday sun gangs ay sweetest down,
My bonnie boys leave their wark i' the town ;
My heart loups light at my ain ingle side,
Whan my kin' blythe bairn-time is a sitting roun'.

The Sabbath morning comes, an' warm lowes the sun,
Ilk heart's fu' o' joy a' the parishen roun';
Round the hip o' the hill comes the sweet Psalm-tune,
An' the auld fowk a' to the preaching are bowne.

The hearts o' the younkers loup lightsome, to see
The gladness which dwalls in their auld grannie's ee ;
An' they gather i' the sun, 'side the green haw-tree,
Nae new-flown birds are sae mirthsome an' hie.

Tho' my sonsie dame's cheeks nae to auld age are prief,
Tho' the roses which blumed there are smit i' the leaf;
Tho' the young blinks o' luve hae a' died in her ee,
She is bonnier an' dearer than ever to me !

Ance Poortith came in 'yont our hallan to keek,
But my Jeanie was nursing an' singing sae sweet,
That she laid down her powks at anither door cheek,
An' steppit blythely ben her auld shanks for to beek.

My hame is the mailen weel stockit an' fu,
My bairns are the flocks an' the herds which I loo ;—
My Jeanie is the gowd an' delight o' my ee,
She's worth a hale lairdship o' mailens to me !

O wha wad fade awa like a flower i' the dew,
An' nae leave a sprout for kind heaven to pu' ?
Wha wad rot 'mang the mools, like the trunk o' the tree,
Wi' nae shoots the pride o' the forest to be !

The following unpublished verses contain a kindred sentiment with the preceding. The reader will be curious to see the same subject treated by a mere peasant, and by an elegant and accomplished living writer, Mrs. Elizabeth Hamilton, author of "The Cottagers of Glenburnie."

MY AIN FIRE-SIDE.

O, I hae seen great anes, and been in great ha's,
'Mang Lords and 'mang Ladies a' cover'd wi' braws;
At feasts made for Princes, wi' Princes I've been,
Whar the great shine o' splendour has dazzled my een.
But a sight sae delightfu' I trow I ne'er spied,
As the bonnie blythe blink o' my ain fire-side;
   My ain fire-side, my ain fire-side,
    Oh, cheering's the blink o' my ain fire-side!

Ance mair, Guid be thankit! by my ain heartsome ingle,
Wi' the friends o' my youth I cordially mingle:
Nae form to compel me to seem wae or glad,
I may laugh when I'm merry—and sigh when I'm sad;
Nae fausehood to dreed, and nae malice to fear,
But truth to delight me—and friendship to cheer.—
Of a' roads to happiness ever was tried,
There's nane half sae sure as ane's ain fire-side,
   Ane's ain fire-side, ane's ain fire-side,
    Oh! happiness sits by ane's ain fire-side!

When I draw in my stool on my cozie hearth-stane,
My heart loups sae light, I scarce ken't for my ain ;
Care's flown on the winds—it's clean out o' sight,
Past sorrows they seem but as dreams o' the night ;
I hear but kent voices ;—kent faces I see,
And mark fond affection glint saft frae ilk ee.
Nae fleechings o' flattery—nae boastings o' pride,
'Tis heart speaks to heart, at ane's ain fire-side ;
   My ain fire-side, my ain fire-side,
   Oh ! there's nought to compare to my ain fire-side !

———————

As the plaintive and amatory songs are now completed, we cannot dismiss them without taking notice of their bold, original, and strongly-marked character. There are no quaint allusions, nor covert indelicacy. Although they come within the short arm-grips of love, and abound with glowing kisses and clasps of ardent affection, yet they everywhere retain a chastened respect that accords with the delicacy of the female mind. That sacred confidence which they have in private love-meetings is the true mark of a virtuous mind, and is peculiar to the character of the Scottish maidens. The inner fences of modesty and virtue which incase the heart, they hold inviolable, though their unsuspecting innocence sometimes leaves the outer works unguarded.

These songs contain fine pictures of rustic wooing, faithfully drawn from real life. They are a little touched with the romantic spirit of chivalry, but this gives them a higher and more dignified aspect.

The Persons who present themselves are none of the fabled Arcadians :—shepherds and shepherdesses who do nothing but pipe to their sheep, or plait garlands for their hair. Nor have these pastorals an exuberance of roses and lilies, like our courtly English ones, whose swains and nymphs resemble lords and ladies parading among their vassals at the rental time, who never smear sheep, or blister their gloved hands with shepherds' crooks. Nor are there any of the apparatus of classical deification :—cloven-footed Pans, satyrs, sylphs, and dryads, with all the light infantry of fairy freaks, or bedlam personification. The broad, but exquisite Doric of these reliques, is not obscured by the antique foppery of heathen mythology : they have nothing of foreign growth : —all is Scottish—language and ideas. The lads and lasses are pure flesh and blood ; homely, every-day folks. Their kissings and clasping are with earthly lips, and mortal arms. The eloquence of their love is strongly impressed with Scottish feelings, and beautifully embroidered with the Scottish language, as it is spoken in Nithsdale and part of Galloway.

Some acquaintance with the manners and customs of the peasantry is absolutely necessary to have a relish of all the beauties of these pastorals ; yet there is a portion of them that will be understood and admired by every person :—that part which belongs to the general outline of character which runs through all mankind.

G

SONGS

OF

THE NITHSDALE AND GALLOWAY PEASANTRY.

CLASS II.—HUMOROUS.

THE PAWKY AULD KIMMER.*

(NITHSDALE AND GALLOWAY).

I.

THERE'S a pawky auld Kimmer wons low i' the glen ;
Nane kens how auld Kimmer maun fecht and maun fen ;
Kimmer gets maut, and Kimmer gets meal,
And cantie lives Kimmer, right couthie an' hale ;
Kimmer gets bread, an' Kimmer gets cheese,
An' Kimmer's uncannie een keep her at ease.
  " I rede ye speak lowne, lest Kimmer should hear ye ;
  Come sain† ye, come cross ye, an' Gude be near ye !"

II.

Kimmer can milk a hale loan of kye,
Yet sit at the ingle fu' snug an' fu' dry ;
Kimmer a brown cowte o' poor *Laurie* made,
Whan she posted to *Locherbrigg* last Hallowmas rade.‡
Kimmer can sit i' the coat tails o' the moon,
And tipple gude wine at Brabant brewin'.
  " I rede ye speak lowne, lest Kimmer should hear ye ;
  Come sain ye, come cross ye, an' Gude be near ye !"

---

* See the Appendix (E) on Witchcraft.

† *To sain,* to bless.
      " Bess *sain'd herself*, cry'd, ' Lord, be here !'
      And near-hand fell a-swoon for fear."
                        THE MONK AND THE MILLER'S WIFE.

‡ This procession will be explained in the Appendix (E).

III.

Kimmer can sit an' say,—" E'en be 't sae !"
An' red jowes* the Nith atween banking an' brae;
Kimmer can cast owre it her cantraips an' spells,
An' feerie † can cross it in twa braid cockle shells.
The Laird spake to Kimmer for his barren ladie,
An' soon gaed my ladie coats kilted fu' hie.
  " I rede ye speak lowne, lest Kimmer should hear ye;
  Come sain ye, come cross ye, an' Gude be near ye !"

IV.

Kimmer was nae bidden whan the cannie wives gade,
But for Kimmer they ran, an' for Kimmer they rade :
Kimmer an' I are right couthie an' kin'
Or the Laird's ae daughter wad ne'er hae been mine :
I creeshed weel Kimmer's loof wi' howdying fee,
Or a cradle had ne'er a been totched‡ for me !
  " I rede ye speak lowne, lest Kimmer should hear ye;
  Come sain ye, come cross ye, an' Gude be near ye !"

This curious old song belongs to those times of witch-craft and delusion of which there are many vestiges among the peasantry to this day. There are "pawkie auld Kimmers" who can live by their "uncannie een," in many parishes of the Scottish Lowlands.

---

* *Jowes*, moves violently.   † *Feerie*, cleverly, actively.
‡ *Totching* is the act of rocking the cradle gently with the foot.

There is a story of one of these dames having meal, barley, cheese, &c., sent her to make her *een look kindly*, and to compound for spoiled butter and elf-shot kye. Many marvels would be related in this place of these cantraip dames, had not the genius of discretion, at this critical moment, overshadowed the Editor and his papers, whispering in his ear,—

"I rede ye *speak lowne*, lest *Kimmer* should hear ye ;
Come sain ye, come cross ye, an' Gude be near ye !"

THE EWE-BUGHTS.*

This song was communicated to the Editor by his friend Allan Cunningham, who learned it when a boy, from a servant-girl belonging to his father, an honest, cultivated farmer, an acquaintance and neighbour of Burns, when he lived at Ellisland. He never heard any one sing it but herself.

I

THE lark dried his dewy wings i' the sun,
  Aboon the rigs o' barley,
Whan a bonnie lad came to my window bredd
  Wi' me to haud a parley :
O are ye sleeping, my bonnie, bonnie lass,
  Or are ye wauken I' ferlie ?†
Will ye rise an' come to the faulds wi' me,
  Our ewes are bleating sairlie ?

---

* " In a MS. account of Selkirkshire, by Mr. John Hodge, dated 1722, in the Advocates' Library, he adds a circumstance which has now become antiquated: ' That there was then to be seen, at Tait's Cross, *boughted*, and milked, upwards of twelve thousand ewes, in the month of June, about eight o'clock at night, at one view." *Boughted* is a verb, formed from the substantive *bought*, or *bught*, which meant a fold for ewes, while they were milked."

CHALMERS' CALEDONIA, Vol. 11. (Note, p. 973.

† *I ferlie*, 1 wonder.

II.

First I pat on my jupes sae green,
  An' kilted my coaties rarely ;
Awa I gaed but stockings or shoon
  Amang the dews sae pearlie !
He played his hand 'mang my lang brown hair,
  An' kittled my white cheek fairlie,
Till his een o'erbrimmed wi' kin', kin' luve,
  An' haith ! I pitied him sairlie.

III.

The sun it raise, an' better raise,
  An' owre the hills lowed rarely ;*
The wee lark sang, an' higher sang
  Aboon the bearded barley.
We touzled sae lang on the sunny knowe-side,
  Whare the gowan-heads hang pearlie,
That the bluidy, bluidy Tod† had worried a' the faul
  An' left my lad fu' barely.

---

* *Lowed*, blazed.   † *Tod*, the fox.

H

THE PAWKY LOON, THE MILLER.

I.

YOUNG Peggy's to the mill gane
  To sift her daddie's meller;
A kindlie maid I trow she was;—
  A pawky loon the miller!
An' she coost aff her high heel'd shoon,
  Laced down wi' thread o' siller;
O maiden, kilt your kirtle high,
  Quo' the young pawky miller.

II.

The new-meal flushed the lassie's cheek,
  Ere the black cock was crawing;
An' luve began to light her ee,
  By the ruddie morn was dawing.
O dight, quo' she, yere mealy mou',
  For my twa lips yere drauking;
But the pawky loon he keppit the words
  Wi' his clapping and his smacking.

III.

Young Peggy has unkilt her coat,
  An' hame she's gane fu' cheerlie;
Aften she dighted her bonnie mealy mou,
  An' lilted awa' fu' clearlie:—

Dustie is the miller's coat,
 An' dustie is the colour ;
An' mealie was the sweet, sweet kiss
 Which I gat frae the miller !*

IV.

O what has keeped ye, Peggy lass,
 At sifting o' the meller ?
An' what has tuffled yere gowden locks,
 Kepped up wi' kame o' siller ?
An hae ye been licking the mouter, lass,
 Or kissing the dusty miller ? †

V.

A pawky cat came frae the mill, ee—
 Wi' a bonnie, bowsie tailie,
An' it whiskit it cross my lips I trow,
 Which made them a' sae mealie.
An' three gude dams ran down the trows,
 Before was grun' the meller.
An' I'm gaun back for shellen seeds
 To the young pawkie miller !

---

* This verse used to be greatly admired by Burns, for its characteristic and forcible expression. It may be found in an old song of little merit, in the *Musical Museum*.

† In singing, the two last lines of this verse are repeated.

This old song has been long admired and sung by the peasantry.   There were many variations of it ; this is the best that could be found.   It was transmitted by the young girl who has preserved so many reliques of Nithsdale and Galloway song.   These are her words addressed to a Scottish poet.

*   *   *   *   " With regard to Peggy's *kilted coats*, our right is just this—' *Kilt them up,*' quo' the auld wife, ' *to the tying o' yere garters.*'   Prudery herself could not object to this.   But these high-kilted days are past, and the gude auld unthinking customs of our ancestors appear indelicate to a refined mind.   Should Peggy's kilted coats be too high for your bardship's second-sighted een, I beseech you let down a trowse or twa o' them yoursel', and don't let the nakedness of our lasses' legs offend the more delicate een of their granddaughters.

" Is it of use to tell you that I have known this old song from my infancy sung by the old dames trained in the homely school of *broad local manners ?*   Indeed they frequently sung higher-kilted songs than this, with as much modesty perhaps as the trained ladies sing the smoother lipping verses of modern politeness.

" Ramsay says, in the preface to his *Tea-Table Miscellany*, that he has kept out all smut and ribaldry.   The volumes bear evidence, according to modern manners, against him.   This is instance enough that our manners, and customs, and opinions are altered."

The above remarks lead to a question at once curious and difficult of solution ; perhaps there are not two men living who would decide alike upon it.   The taste of the present age rejects as gross and indelicate those free compositions which our ancestors not only countenanced but admired.   The tales of Chaucer ; the scenes of Massinger, of Beaumont and Fletcher, and even of Shakspeare, would not be tolerated in a modern poet ; and if the applause with which those compositions were received be a test of their merit, we must conclude that they were faithful pictures of the manners of those times, and hence we may be ready to congratulate ourselves, that the progress of virtue has kept pace with that of refinement.   Yet, in fact, the morals of our forefathers were as strict and perhaps purer and sounder than our own ; and we have been taught to look up to them as genuine models of the honest, incorruptible character of Englishmen.   They were strangers indeed to delicacy of taste ; they beheld the broad and unpruned delineations of nature, and thought no harm ; while we, on the most distant approach to freedom of thought and expression, turn away in disgust, and vehemently express our displeasure.   Does this arise from the irritable shame of guilt, or from the sensibility of innocence ? Perhaps not wholly from either, but from a cautious apprehension that the obduracy of vice may be brazened into impudence by the perversion of a satire which is aimed to expose it ; and from a sense of the difficulty which unquestionably exists, of preserving the purity of a rising generation unsullied, in this luxurious and refined age, when the allurements of vice are so various, and the path of virtue is so beset with temptation.   For the evil affections of the mind, as well as for those of the body, prevention is easier than cure ; and the same feeling which prompts

the father of a family to guard his children from every
immoral incitement, actuates the censors of literature,
and the audiences of our theatres, to banish from the
press and from the stage, those productions which tend,
however indirectly and remotely, to cherish licentious-
ness. Human nature is ever the same, but society is
always progressive, and at every stage of refinement the
passions require stricter control ; not because they are
more violent, but because the circumstances which excite
them are multiplied. Hence we might almost be
tempted to envy the secure and unsuspecting innocence
of our ancestors, for in this sense the maxim of the poet
is strictly just :

————— Where ignorance is bliss,
'Tis folly to be wise.

And if we trace back the progress of society to its
primitive state we shall find, that the innocence of mankind is in an inverse ratio to their advancement in knowledge. The inhabitants of Otaheite were comparatively
virtuous, so long as the waves of the Pacific preserved
them from the contagion of European intercourse ; and
the pictures which have been drawn of their simple and
guileless manners, remind us of the state of our first
parents in Paradise before the fall :—" And they were
both naked, the man and the woman, and were not
ashamed."

THE GRAY COCK.

A stanza of this romantic little song has for many years
been thrust into the verses beginning,

" Saw ye my father, or saw ye my mother."

Its richness and difference of rhyme soon convince us
that it belongs to better company. Pinkerton has
printed these spurious words six and twenty years ago,
in his *Select Scottish Ballads* ; and though he pronounced
even them, to constitute " an excellent song of superla-
tive beauty," yet from that time to the present no exertions have been made to recover the original glowing
verses now presented to the reader. It appears that his
copy was popular in England at the time he published.
The air has a correspondent beauty with the words : the
composer of it is, I believe, unknown. This copy was
communicated by Mr. Allan Cunningham. He had it
from his father, whose memory was richly fraught with
old songs, and notices regarding them. He used to
point out the inequality of the song as it stood in various
collections, and repeat this as the precious relique of the
original. The *auld Guid-Wife* awakened by the cock,
and hearing the wooer steal away—the girl's archly-simple
reply, come deeply into the mysteries of Scottish wooing.
Their songs abound with traits of this kind :

Wha patters sae late at our gyle window !
　　Mither, its the cauld sleet ;
Come in yere wa's, quo' the sleeky guid-wife,
　　An' warm thae frozen feet.

THE GRAY COCK.

I.

I'LL clip, quo' she, yere lang gray wing,
　　An' pouk yere rosie kame,
If ye daur tak the gay morn-star
　　For the morning's ruddie leam ! *
But if ye craw na till the day,
　　I'll make yere bauk o' silk,
And ye shall pickle the red cherries,
　　And drink the reeking milk !

II.

Flee up, flee up, my bonnie gray cock,
　　An' craw whan it is day ;
An' I'll make ye a kame o' the beaten gowd,
　　An' yere wings o' the siller gray !
But fause, fause proved the bonnie gray cock,
　　An hour owre soon crew he ;
He clappit his wings owre the auld guid-wife,
　　And an angry wife raise she.

---

* To *leam*, to blaze, to gleam :—
　　　" And a' the land seemed in a *leam*."
　　　　　　　　　　　BARBOUR'S BRUS.

III.

Wha's that, quo' she, at our door latch,
   Is it some limmer loun?
Na, mither, it is the pawky tod
   That howls again' the moon.
What step is that by our ha' en',
   Which treads sae light o' spauld? *
O mither, it is the herd laddie,
   Gaun by to look the fauld!

---

* *Sae light o' spauld,* so light of foot.

I

STARS, DINNA KEEK IN.

I.

STARS, dinna keek in,
And see me wi' Marie;
And O, thou bonnie, bonnie moon,
Don't in our window tarrie!
O yestreen ye scaured me,
O yestreen ye marred me,
Frae monie a kiss ye barred me,
　　Ye keeked sae in on Marie.

II.

Marie's a winsome quean,
My dear Marie!
Weel she loes, she shaws ye loes,
The lad wha loes Marie;
But nae tell-tale moon loes she,
Nor love-prying star loes she;
The session soon enough will see
　　Wha lies wi' Marie.

*　　　　*　　　　*

GALLOWAY TAM

Is a song of several stanzas. In the *Scots Musical Museum* there are only two verses of it published. Johnson has either not known the whole of it, or, as is usual with him, he has cast the best parts adrift. The Editor has recovered and united the two last humorous verses to their fellows. " O ignorance parts gude companie !"

O GALLOWAY Tam came here to woo,
I'd rather we'd gi'en him the bawsand cow ;
For our lass Bess may curse and ban
The wanton wit o' Galloway Tam !

O Galloway Tam came here to shear,
I'd rather we'd gi'en him the gude gray mere ;
He kiss'd the gudewife and dang the gudeman,
And that's the tricks o' Galloway Tam !

Galloway Tam rides far and near,
There's nane can graith wi' siccan gear ;
The lowns ca' out, wha sing the Psalm,
"Room i' the stool* for Galloway Tam !"

The Howdie† lifts frae the Beuk her ee,
Says " blessings light on his pawkie ee !"
An' she mixes maist i' the holie Psalm,
"O Davie ‡ thou were't like Galloway Tam !"

* Of Repentance.   † *Howdie*, the midwife.
‡ *Davie*, the Psalmist.

TAM BO.

WILL ye fee wi' me, Tam Bo, Tam Bo?
Will ye fee wi' me, my heart and my Jo?
And ye'se be at hamelike my tae ee,
If ye'll fee wi' a pitifu' widow like me.

Ye'se get merks three, Tam Bo, Tam Bo,
Ye'se get merks three, my heart and my Jo!
And is nae that a dainty bit fee,
To get frae a pitifu' widow like me?

Ye'se get bairns' meat, Tam Bo, Tam Bo,
Ye'se get bairns' meat, my heart and my Jo!
Saps o' cream, and gude beef-bree,
If ye'll fee wi' a pitifu' widow like me.

Ye'se get waled wark, Tam Bo, Tam Bo,
Ye'se get waled wark, my heart and my Jo!
Ye'se faugh our gudeman's weel-plowed lea,
If ye'll fee wi' a pitifu' widow like me.

And if ye do't weel, Tam Bo, Tam Bo,
And if ye do't weel, my heart and my Jo,
For every merk ye sall hae three;
Will ye fee wi' a pitifu' widow like me?

"I canna lie my lane, my lane,
I canna lie my lane, my lane,
Tho' I brawlie can faugh yere weel plowed lea,
Or there's nane can do't i' the hale Kintrie.

Ye'se lie wi' me, Tam Bo, Tam Bo,
Ye'se lie wi' me, my heart and my Jo,
Hae! there's airle-pennies twa or three,
Come hame wi' a pitifu' widow like me.

The northwind's cauld, Tam Bo, Tam Bo,
The northwind's cauld, my heart and my Jo!
It freezed the drap in our Johnnie's bleer'd ee,
O kind was the news it blew to me!

The southwind's sweet, Tam Bo, Tam Bo,
The southwind's sweet, my heart and my jo!
It wags the gowans on our gude-man's bree,
And dries the tears frae my pitifu' ee.

WERE YE AT THE PIER O' LEITH?

WERE ye at the Pier o' Leith?
  Or came in by Bannochie?
Crossed ye at the boat o' Craig?—
  Saw ye the lad wha courted me?
Short hose an' belted plaidie,
  Garters tyed below his knee;
O he was a bonnie lad,
  The blythe lad wha courted me!

O weary fa' the lang yellow broom,
  Gaur'd me gang kilted to the knee,
May the sleekie bird ne'er build a nest
  That sung to see the hawk wi' me!

      *   *   *   *

OUR GUID-WIFE'S AY IN THE RIGHT.

(FROM MRS. COPLAND.)

I.

Our guid-wife's ay in the right,
　　Ay in the right, ay in the right,
Our guid-wife's ay in the right,
　　And I am ay in the wrang, Jo !
Right or wrang she's ay in the right ;
　　She's ay in the right, she's ay in the right ;
Right or wrang she's ay in the right,
　　And I am ay in the wrang, Jo !

II.

There's gowans grow at our kirk wa',
　　At our kirk wa', at our kirk wa',
Owre monie a dinsome Carlin law*
　　Fu' blythe to win aboon, Jo !
Wad ance that winsome Carle Death,
　　But rowe her in his black mort-claith,†·
I'd make a wadset o' an aith
　　To feast the parishen, Jo !

---

* *Law*, low.

† *Mort Claith*, is a covering of black velvet, spread over the coffin at ：
funeral.

ORIGINAL OF BURNS'S CARLE OF KELLY-BURN BRAES.

THERE was an auld man was hauding his plow,
    Hey! an' the rue grows bonnie wi' thyme!
By came the Devil, says, "How do ye do?"
    An' the thyme it is withered, an' the rue is in prime.

It's neither your ox, nor your ass that I crave,
    Hey-! an' the rue grows bonnie wi' thyme!
But your auld scaulding wife, man, and her I maun
    have,
    An' the thyme it is withered, an' the rue is in prime.

"Go take her, go take her," the auld carle said,
    Hey! an' the rue grows bonnie wi' thyme!
Ye'll no keep her lang, an' that I'm afraid,
    An' the thyme it is withered, an' the rue is in prime.

The Devil he mounted her on his back,
    Hey! an' the rue grows bonnie wi' thyme!
An' awa like a pedlar he trudged wi' his pack,
    An' the thyme it is withered, an' the rue is in prime.

He carried her on till he came to hell's door,
    Hey! an' the rue grows bonnie wi' thyme!
An' bade her gae in, for a bitch an' a whore,
    An' the thyme it is withered, an' the rue is in prime.

He placed her on his big arm chair,
  Hey ! an' the rue grows bonnie wi' thyme !
An' thousands o' devils came roun' her to stare,
  An' the thyme it is withered, an' the rue is in prime.

But ay as they at the auld carlin played pouk,
  Hey ! an' the rue grows bonnie wi' thyme !
She gied them a bann, an' she lent them a clout,
  An' the thyme it is withered, an' the rue is in prime.

A reekit wee devil gloured owre the wa',
  Hey ! an' the rue grows bonnie wi' thyme !
Says, help ! master, help ! or she'll ruin us a',
  An' the thyme it is withered, an' the rue is in prime.

The deil he came up wi' a good brunstane rung,
  Hey ! an' the rue grows bonnie wi' thyme !
An' out at the door the auld carlin he swung,
  An' the thyme it is withered, an' the rue is in prime.

He hynt up the carlin again on his back,
  Hey ! an' the rue grows bonnie wi' thyme !
An' awa fu' blythely he trudged wi' his pack,
  An' the thyme it is withered, an' the rue is in prime.

He carried her owre an acre or two,
  Hey ! an' the rue grows bonnie wi' thyme !
Till he came to the auld man hauding his plow,
  An' the thyme it is withered, an' the rue is in prime.

K

An' ay as the auld carle ranted and sang,
  Hey! an' the rue grows bonnie wi' thyme!
"In troth, my auld spunkie, ye'll no keep her lang;"
  An' the thyme it is withered, an' the rue is in prime.

"Gude morrow," most sadly, the auld carle said,
  Hey! an' the rue grows bonnie wi' thyme!
"Yere bringing me back my auld wife I'm afraid;"
  An' the thyme it is withered, an' the rue is in prime.

"I tryed her in spunks, and in cau'drons I tryed her,
  Hey! an' the rue grows bonnie wi' thyme!
"An' the wale o' my brunstane wadna hae fry'd her,
  An' the thyme it is withered, an' the rue is in prime.

"I stapped her in the neuk o' my den,"
  Hey! an' the rue grows bonnie wi' thyme!
"But the vera damn'd ran, when the carlin gaed ben,"
  An' the thyme it is withered, an' the rue is in prime.

"Sae here's a gude pose * for to keep her yoursel',
  Hey! an' the rue grows bonnie wi' thyme!
"She's nae fit for heaven, an' she'll ruin a' hell,"
  An' the thyme it is withered, an' the rue is in prime.

---

* *Pose*, or *hoard of money*, a purseful of coin. "He has a guid pose," is an old expression for riches. "A pose o' gowd," occurs in an old song, which I do not at present recollect.

This original and strongly relieved song was retouched by Burns. Yet there is reason to believe he had not seen the whole of the verses which constitute the present copy, as it contains many characteristic traits, that his critical taste would have held sacred.

A truly ludicrous and witty vein of wedded strife enlivens many fragments of Scottish song :

> Souter Sawney had a wife,
> Souter Sawney had a wife,
> Souter Sawney had a wife,
>   They ca'd her Meg the Randie:
> She suppit the butter off Sawney's brose,
> She suppit the butter off Sawney's brose,
> And wadset baith his sark an' hose,
>   For burning sowps o' brandy.
>
> She rampit butt, she rampit ben,
> Wi' cock broo in a frything pan ;
> It dreeped down Sawney's meezled shin,
>   " Hech ! Cuckold, did I scaud you ! "
> The donnort bodie croon'd right lowne,
> Whyle tears dreeped a' his black beard down,
> " The deil maun knuckle to yere tune,
>   Or hell it winna haud you ! "

The honest carle of " *Kellyburn Braes*," seems to have possessed all the patience of *Souter Sawney;* yet the Souter, though he " *crooned right lowne* " before his unmanageable shrew, would at times gratulate himself in her absence, with a verse of

FAIRLY SHOT ON HER.

I.

O gin I were fairly shot on her,
O gin I were fairly shot on her,
Auld Satan wad lie neither side nor on top on her,
But wad cowre in his cleugh, and sing—"fairly shot
    on her."

II.

When I sing at the Beuk she will lilt like a starling,
" Johnnie come kiss me, my Joe and my darling ;"
O gin the grass wad grow green on the top on her,
I'd rin daft wi' joy were I fairly shot on her.

III.

Auld Clootie, thous't had a han' i' the getting her,
Or she'd choked wi' the broo, whilk they took for to
    christen her,
The lugs o' a tinkler wad deave for to listen her,
O gin I were fairly shot on her.

Did not his respect for the fair dames of Nithsdale
and Galloway restrain the Editor, he could present them
with many more lamentable fragments of hen-pecked
ejaculation ; but this sad remnant of the olden time having now no modern parallel, it would be deemed invidi-
ous and uncharitable in him (conscious of owing so
much to these ladies), to visit the sins of the mothers
upon their daughters of the gentler generation.

THE ORIGINAL OF BURNS'S "GUDE ALE COMES," &c.

O GUDE ale comes an' gude ale goes,
Gude ale gaurs me sell my hose ;
Sell my hose and pawn my shoon,
Gude ale keeps my heart aboon.

Gude ale keeps me bare and bizzy,
Gaurs me tipple till I be dizzy ;
An' keep a soup till the afternoon —
Gude ale keeps my heart aboon.

Our guidwife coft a snip white coat,
Wi' monie a weel hained butter-groat,
But it's a wadset* i' the town —
Gude ale keeps my heart aboon.

---

* *A wadset*—a pledge. To *wad*, or *wed*, is to lay in pledge. Thus Burns—

> " Here's that little *wadset*,
> Butle's scrap o' truth ;
> Pawned in a gin shop,
> Quenching holie drouth."

Sometimes it means *to bet*.

> " Wad ance that wynsome Carle Death
> But rowl her in his black mort-claith ;
> I'd make a *wadset* o' an aith,
> To feast the parishen, Jo."
>
> OLD SONG, p. 71.

I had sax owsen in a pleugh,
They drew a' weel enough;
I selled them a' just ane by ane,
Gude ale keeps my heart aboon.

I keepit sax groats for twa lang weeks,
Till they must brunt my hoddin-breeks;
But I slokened the limmers ane by ane,
Gude ale keeps my heart aboon.

Gude ale's the medicine aft spaed * of,
The very stuff that life is made of;
Drapt in a receipt frae the moon,
To keep men's sinking hearts aboon.

----

* Foretold.

THERE'S NANE O' THEM A' LIKE MY BONNIE LASS.

(GALLOWAY.)

This old song cost much pains in collecting. The first, second, third, and fifth verses are from the young girl who recited "Derwentwater." The fourth verse, and part of the sixth, are from Mrs. Copland; the last verses are restored from those ewe-bughting and trysting sing-ings, once so common in Nithsdale and Galloway.

There were mixed with it several verses of middling merit. It is here presented to public notice, for the first time, in a perfect form.

Nithsdale and the skirts of Galloway equally claim this song; it is known in both, and is much admired in the rude and unwinnowed way in which it is usually sung.

I'LL part wi' a' ere I part wi' my lassie,
I'll part wi' a' ere I part wi' my lassie;
The ladies o' Nithsdale are proud, high, an' saucy,
But there's nane o' them a' like my bonnie lassie.

Her twa rosy lips are like kame-drappit hinney,
Her twa laughing een amang lads are uncanny;

Her links o' black hair owre her shouthers fa' bonnie,
An' where's there a maiden like my bonnie Jeanie !

White is the han' o' my ain bonnie lassie,
Leal is her heart, fu' o' kindness my lassie ;
Yestreen i' my arms how she drappit, fu' gawcie,
" I'll ay be ye're ain," quo' my bonnie young lassie.

She has nae gude mailens to haud her ay easy,
Nor pearlins nor gowd to make her look gawcie ;
She has nae braw claes for to shine i' the causie,
But there's nane o' them a' like my bonnie lassie.

My friends they are proud, an' my mither is saucy,
My auld auntie tauks ay the crown o' the causie ;
But here's my JEAN's health i' the siller-lipped tassie !
I'll part wi' them a' e'er I part wi' my lassie.

Frae the cot to the faulding I've followed my lassie,
To kirk and to market I gang wi' my lassie ;
Up the warlock glen, down the boglie causie,
An' thro' a' the warld I'd follow my lassie.

Fu' rich is thy heart in leal kindness, my lassie,
Tho' hamely thy claithing, yet aught sets my lassie ;
Thou art a new pearl, in gowd I will case ye,
An' next to my heart, O ! for ever I will place ye.

I'll part wi' a' e'er I part wi' my lassie,
I'll part wi' a' e'er I part wi' my lassie ;
I'll tauk wi' my auntie the crown o' the causie,
An' shaw me the lad wha will hae sic a lassie!

MY KIMMER AND I.

This song seems to be a slip, or scion from " Todlin'
Hame." It is but modern.

WHAN Kimmer and I were groom and bride,
We had twa pint stoups at our bed-side ;
Sax times fu' and sax times dry,
An' raise for drouth—my Kimmer and I.

My Kimmer and I gade to the fair,
Wi' twal pun' Scots in sarking to ware ;
But we drank the gude brown hawkie dry,
An' sarkless hame came Kimmer an' I.

My Kimmer and I gade to the town,
For wedding-breeks an' a wedding gown ;
But the sleeky auld priest he wat our eye
In sackcloth gowns—my Kimmer an' I.

My Kimmer and I maun tak the Beuk,
Wi' a twal pint stoup in our peat neuk ;
Ere the psalm be done, the dish is dry,
An' drouthelie pray my Kimmer an' I.

My Kimmer and I are scant o' claes,
Wi' soups o' drink and soups o' brose,

L

But late we rise and soon gae lie,
And cantilie live—my Kimmer and I.

My Kimmer is auld, my Kimmer is bent,
And I'm gaun louting owre a kent; *
The well o' life is dribbling dry,
An' drouthie, drouthie's Kimmer an' I.

---

* *To lout owre a kent,* to stoop, to bend double with age, supported by a long staff.

VARIATIONS OF "TIBBIE FOWLER."

In the *Trystes* of Nithsdale there are many variations of
this curious song. Some of them have been long forgotten. Those here recovered are given from the
various recitations which the Editor has picked up, from
a diligent search among the old people of Nithsdale.
They exhibit a fine proof of the taste and abilities of the
peasantry.

THE brankit lairds o' Gallowa,
The hodden breeks o' Annan Water,
The bonnets blue of fair Nithsdale,
Are 'yont the hallan wooing at her.

Tweed-shaw's tarry neives are here,
Braksha' gabs frae Moffat Water,
An' half the thieves o' Annandale
Are come to steal her gear, and daute her.

I mind her weel in plaiden gown,
Afore she got her uncle's coffer ;
The gleds might pyked her at the dyke,
Before the lads wad shored them off her.

Now she's got a bawsent cowte,
Graithing sewed wi' thread o' siller;
Silken sonks to haud her doup,
And half the kintra's trystin' till her.

———

Sour plumbs are gude wi' sugar baked—
Slaes are sweet wi' kames o' hinnie;
The bowltest carlin i' the land,
Gowd can make her straught and bonnie.

———

I wadna gie twa rosie lips,
Wi' breath like mixed milk and honey;
Which i' the gloamin' dew I kissed,
For Tibbie wi' a mine o' monie.

———

I wadna gie the haffet locks,
Wi' blobs o' dew sae richly drapping;
Which lay yestreen upon my breast,
For Tibbie wi' her ladie happing.*

---

* TIBBIE FOWLER.

(THE OLD WORDS.)

Tibbie Fowler o' the glen,
  There's o'er mony wooin at her,
Tibbie Fowler o' the glen,
  There's o'er mony wooin at her,
Wooin at her, pu'in at her,
  Courtin at her, canna get her,
Filthy elf, its for her pelf,
  That a' the lads are wooin at her.

To shew how these *Trystes* would alter the original cast of a song, we will give some stray verses picked up while in search of others. It was customary for the young men of neighbouring parishes to come to the public Trystes, and sing. Sometimes feuds of bloody termination subsisted between parishes, which were mutually kindled at these mixed meetings, where strokes of native satire, nicknames of satirical allusion, and reproach of ancestry and character, would mingle in the conversation, and in song. As a specimen, the following verses may be given, grafted on *Tibbie Fowler*. Two

---

Ten cam east, and ten cam west,
  Ten cam rowin o'er the water ;
Twa cam down the lang-dyke side,
  There's twa and thirty wooin at her.
    Wooin at her, &c.

There's seven but, and seven ben,
  Seven in the pantry wi' her ;
Twenty head about the door,
  There's ane and forty wooin at her.
    Wooin at her, &c.

She's got pendles in her lugs,
  Cockle shells wad set her better :
High-heel'd shoon, and siller tags,
  And a' the lads are wooin at her.
    Wooin at her, &c.

Be a lassie e'er sae black,
  An' she hae the name o' siller,
Set her upo' *Tintock** tap,
  The wind will blaw a man till her.
    Wooin at her, &c.

---

* *Tintock*, a stupendous hill near the town of Biggar.

lads of Dunscore parish, coming to a Kirkmahoe Tryste,
had this witty verse interpolated in its proper place—

" The Dunscore ' *Salt Lairds* ' stilt the Nith,
    And muddie a' our supper water ;
The gray-beard solemn-leaguing lowns
    Thraw by the beuk o' God to dawte her.
The birds hae a' forhood* their nests,
    The trouts hae ta'en the Cairn and Annan,
For hoddin breeks and stilting shanks,
    Between the sun-set and the dawin'."

These lines were instantly retorted by this blithesome
effort of local parish pleasantry,

" Kirmahoe louped on her sonks,
    Wi' new creeshed shoon and weel darned hosen ;
And cry'd to maw an acre kail,
    And hing the pan wi' water brose on ;
And wha will lend us brydal gear,
    Sheep amang the kale to simmer,
Gullies for to sheer their cloots,
    Swats to foam aboon the timmer."

Be a lassie e'er sae fair,
    An' she want the pennie siller,
A flie may fell her in the air,
    Before a man be even till her.
        Wooin at her, &c.

* *Forhood*, forsaken.

Dunscore sent her spauls o' sheep,
Lent her owre our big brose ladle ;
Pewter plates and hansel gear,
To mense her wi' at Tibbie's brydal.
Ye've pyked the banes o' yere leap-year's cow,
Yere aught day's kale's a' finished fairly ;
Yere big brose pot has nae played brown
Sin' the Reaver Rade o' *gude Prince Charlie.*

An old Nithsdale farmer possessed a fair portion of
that satiric humour which belongs to the song of *Tibbie
Fowler.* Having two daughters "mair black than bonnie," he would hint at their uncomeliness—" My lasses
wad hae mensed me had I lived among the black, but
comelie daughters of Jerusalem," he would say ;—" but
I'll do wi' them as the Gudeman o' Roanshaw did wi'
his cowtes—He put siller graithing on them, and hung
bobbins o' gowd at their manes, and shawed them at the
market, saying—' Some will gie a bode for ye, for the
sonks and bridle !' "

CANNIE WI' YOUR BLINKIN', BESSIE.

Tune—" Willie was a Wanton Wag."

This very modern song seems to have been erected by
some poor bard to the memory of the many rubs and
jeers he had experienced on his first outset among the
young witches of Galloway.

———

Love has set my saul on fire,
　　Bessie, ye hae blawn the bleeze ;
A' the neebors round conspire
　　Night an' day my life to teaze.

Cannie wi' your blinkin', Bessie,
　　Beet nae mair the dools I dree ;
Hoolie, hoolie, bonnie lassie,
　　Wi' the glamour o' your ee.

Dreigh and doure I hae been yokit,
　　Since our maiden tryste yestreen,
Whan my heart I first unlockit
　　On the velvet sward sae green.

Lampin *Tibbie Deemster* saw us
　　Tak a kindly kiss or twa ;
Syne awa she bang'd to blaw us,
　　Mumlin what she heard an' saw.

Slaverin' Jock glowr'd owre the hallan,
　　Kindly speir'd for *Wooster Tam* ;
"Swith!" quo he, "ye beardless callan,
　　Tak your beuk, and learn your Psalm."

Scowderdowp came to our dwallin,
　　And wi' serious smudgin' leuk,
Spier'd at Aunty, gin the Callan
　　Wanted either cleps or crook.

'Deed, quo' *Kate*, our Clachan howdie*
　　Rousty eild, taks ill wi' lear,
Bessie's sleek as ony mowdie,
　　They wha cuddle young learn fair."

Fidgin Davie clew his haffit,
　　Hotchin thrang o' crikes an' flaes ;
" Tam," quo' he, " their gibes we'll laugh at,
　　Whan I mak the bairns' claes."

Warst of a', *Rab Birse*, the Souter,
　　Sent it ringin' thro' the town,
How he'd fairly poutch'd the multre
　　O' the weans's bridal shoon.

Blythe hae I been wi' my Bessie,
　　Blyther days I never saw ;
Gaun to woo my bonnie lassie,
　　Through the glens o' Gallowa' !

---

* *The Clachan Howdie*, the village midwife.

M

THE BRIDAL SARK, AND THE BRIDE-GROOM DARG.

(NITHSDALE.)

There is a sort of nursery song in the Pepysian Collection which runs thus,—

> The Elphin Knight sits on a hill,
> Ba, ba, ba, lillie ba;
> He blows his horn both loud and shill,
> The wind hath blown my plaid awa.

This would seem to be the original of these twin songs the " Bridal Sark," and " The Bridegroom Darg." There is a common Scotch song called " Captain Wedderburne's Courtship," much in the same singular and original way. The lady proposes enigmas, which the captain's versatile gallantry soon finds means to solve or to evade.

In these twin songs there is a curious and pleasing collection of Scotch phrases and proverbs, sarcastically chosen and skilfully interspersed to suit the complexion of the songs. This traditionary wisdom has been substituted by some judicious bard for "the wind hath blawn my plaid awa," of the old ballad. Specimens of these national phrases might be given from almost every song and ballad high in public favour. They are full of instruction, conveyed in language often highly figurative and poetical. Aware of their sterling value, Burns has, with his accustomed delicacy of selection, transplanted many of the best and most beautiful into his fields of native poesy, where they will flourish for ever. Those of his songs in particular, which pourtray character, are rich in this proverb lore ; which, heightening their strain of original poetry, endears them to every Scotchman's heart. So estimable indeed do these adages and phrases appear in Scotland, that there is a master proverb to express their value :—

" I'll make proverbs—you make laws."

THE BRIDAL SARK.

Ye may pu' the red gowan that blossoms at Yule,
  (Blaw, blaw, blaw, soft the wind blaw,)
And the gowden-bobb'd lilie that flowers o'er the pool,
  (And the wind it has blawn my plaid awa !)

But a bonnie lass mauna be pu'd till she's ripe,
  (Saft, saft, saft, does the simmer-wind blaw,)
Or she'll melt awa like the snaw frae the dyke,
  (And the ripe lilie-tap i' the sun will fa !)

Gae hame to yer mither, my sonsie young thing,
   (The red, red rose is dawning and a' ;)
Ye'll aulder be, gin the leap year spring,
   (O sweet on the gowan-tap the dew-blobs fa !)

Yere but a young bird wi' the down i' the breast,
   (The purple flower hings on yon abbey wa',)
O'er young to hap i' the twigs roun' the nest,
   (An' sweet frae its tap does the dew-blobs fa !)

Ye may kame down thae gowd-links thae lang simmers
       three,
   (The new paired birds sing blythe i' the shaw,)
And nae yet be fit a bride for to be,
   (O blythe is the sun for he blinks on us a' !)

Thae hands are nae seemlie my sheets for to sew,
   (Whan the red gowans at Yule maun blaw,)
But to wash the burn lilie amang the May-dew,
   (The kirk-yard's ready wi' corses to saw.)

I hae a web of satin at hame,
   (The white haw-bloom drops hinnie an' a',)
Ye maun make me a sark o't a' gowd o' the hem,
   (There's hinney i' the wildest weed that can blaw.)

Ye maun shape it but* sheers, ye maun sew it but silk,
   (There's luve i' the heart tho' the lips say na !)
Ye maun wash it but weet, like a lilie in milk,
   (The rose i' the country ay bonniest does blaw.)

---

* *But*, without.

Ye maun dry't i' the tap o' the new blossom'd thorn,
  (The gray swallow bigs i' the cot-house wa';)
That never had leaves on't since man was born,
  (O I'll pu' the yellow cowslip sae powder'd an' braw.)

The wind mauna touch't, the sun mauna see't,
  (The broom waves yellow whan the simmer winds
      blaw ;)
The dew mauna drop on't, whan laid out to streek,
  (At the heart o' the leal love makes the soonest ca'.)

Ye maun rufflet i' the bosom wi' witch-gowan flower,*
  (The wind wags the rose-tap on our castle wa';)
Ye maun starch't wi' the powther of a pink i' the bower,
  (O the tear-draps o' luve are sweet whan they fa'.)

Ye maun sleeve-button't wi' twa adder-beads,†
  (O Love at my bower-window saftly did ca' ;)

---

* *Witch-gowan flowers* are large yellow gowans, with a stalk filled with pernicious sap, resembling milk, which, when anointed on the eyes, is believed to
cause instaot blindness.   This pernicious juice is called by the peasantry
"Witches' milk."

† *Wi' twa adder beads.*   Adder beads are very rarely found.   According to
popular belief, they are of a beautiful dark grey colour, about two inches in
diameter, with a hole in the centre.   They are the workmanship of the adders,
which assemble to the amount of some hundreds in a certain time of summer, to
cast off their sloughs and renew their age.   They entwist and writhe themselves
among each other until they throw off their last year's sloughs, half melted by
their exertions.   These are all collected and plastered over with frothy saliva,
and again wrought to and fro till they are condensed and shaped into an adder
bead.   Their hissing and noise are frequently heard by the shepherds, when
about their painful act of renovation, and woe to those that approach them.
The bead is often left, and it is treasured up by the shepherds as a talisman of
good luck,   "To make a bead," is a Scottish phrase, applied when a ring of
people is formed on any hurried and important business.

Wi' unchristened fingers maun plait down the breeds,*
(O dinna leave me, lad, till our twa cocks craw.)

Ye maun fauld it and lock it i' the primrose's cup,
(I' the howe-howms o' Nith † my love lives an' a',)
Ye maun row't i' the rose-leaf sealed wi' a dew-drop,
(O the sweet kintra lassie is kindliest of a').

And when ye hae finished this bonnie bride-wark,
(O the lilie wad be bonnie to bloom i' the snaw !)
I'll be yere blythe bridegroom and hansel the sark,
(O the lav'rocks sing loud when the hawk's far awa).

---

* *Wi' unchristened fingers maun plait down the breeds.* This is an allusion to the Scottish BROWNIE, whose unbaptised fingers loved to plait and fit on the ladies' frills.   See the Appendix.

† *I' the howe-howms o' Nith my love lives an' a'.* This line establishes by local testimony a Nithsdale claim to this and the following song. The howe-howms of Nith is a romantic vale, of near ten miles diameter, at the bottom of which stands Dumfries. Cottages, farm-houses, ruined remains of architectural greatness, with gentlemen's seats, beautifully embosomed in plantations, natural and cultivated, with the richness of the harvest fields, form the noblest scene perhaps in the Lowlands of Scotland.

THE BRIDEGROOM DARG.*

(NITHSDALE.)

THE fairest roses fade, which nane ever pu',
    (Blaw, blaw, blaw, saft the wind blaw,)
Though the yellow hinnie hings frae their red rosy
    mou',
    (The wind fa's saft whare the primroses blaw.)

The lealest maidens stand like a rose i' the dew,
    (The wild cushat-doo has nestlings twa,)
And silly man gangs by, nor heeds for to pu',
    (The saft thistle-tap lines the gowdspink's ha'.)

Ye may stand up i' the auld bane dyke,†
    (There's a worm i' the prettiest rose that can
    blaw)
And the corbies will pyke ye afore I be ripe,
    (The young birds sing owre near the hawk's ha'.)

---

* *Darg*, Day's Work.

† "*Ye may stand up i' the auld bane dyke.*" This phrase belongs to a game now much neglected among the Lowland peasantry, called the *Wadds*. Young men and women arranged themselves on each side of the hearth fire, and alternately bestowed husbands and wives on each other. It begins thus :

    " O its hame, an' its hame, an' its hame, hame, hame,
    I think this night I maun gae hame."

The other party cries :

    " Ye had better lycht an' byde a' night,
    An' I'll choose you a bonnie ane."
    " O wha'll chuse an' I wi' ye byde?"
    " I'll gie ye (then name the person) to lie by yere side."

I'll lay ye down 'mang the gowans to streek,
  (I' the deer's den the dog has whalpit an' a')
And turn ye i' the sun, into love it may ye beek ;
  (O the ice i' the beard o' the thistle will thaw.)

I'll wash ye wi' May-dew, i' the neck and the cheek,
  (The bairn maun be washen by the kimmers an
    a',)
They were wat by the priest i' the mirk Monday*
    week,
  (The brocket fac'd cat dights her mou wi' her
    paw.)

If the partner please :
    " I'll set her up on the bonnie pear tree,
    It's straught an' tall, an' sae is she,
    I wad wauke a' night her luve to be."
But if the person proposed be rejected :
    " I'll set her up i' the bank dyke,
    She'll be rotten ere I be ripe,
    The Corbies her auld banes wadna pyke."
This if she be *old*—If she be *young* and rejected :
    " I'll set her up on the high crab-tree,
    Its sour and dowre, an' sae is she ;
    She may gang to the mools unkist by me."

This refusal must be atoned for by a *wadd*, or forfeit. A piece of money, a knife, or any little thing which the owner prizes, and will redeem. His penance of redemption is frequently to kiss those very lips which he had rejected, or any object which is expected to be disagreeable to him. The performance of this loses his *wadd*. This game, I understand, was frequently used to beguile a long winter evening in the cottages of rustics.

  * *Mirk Monday* was a day of almost total darkness, and is frequently counted from as an era. *Windy Saturday* is another of these traditional eras. They are applied as sarcastic reflections on old bachelors or old maids. Thus Burns—

I was owre the lugs in luve wi' yere psalm-singing
    look,
    (There's a black prent Bible i' the reek o' the ha',)
Ye're the half-flayed saint i' the martyrs' book !
    (It's my auld aunt's bolster atween the sheets sma').

I was deep in love, though nae owre far gane,
    (O love's like the dew, it heeds nae where to fa'—)
Wi' death an' his sand-glass on the martyrs'* stane
    (O haffet locks look weel whan they're bleach'd
    like the snaw.)

And a' for the Sark ye hae gien me to sew,
    (My bower is a' wormwood wi' gowd-bolts twa,)
I hae a darg for a bridegroom to do—
    (Wi' a bed o' sweet nettles for to haud lovers twa.)

I hae sax rigs of braid pleugh land,
    (My bride-hood's ready wi' mantle an' a',)
Fenced 'tween the salt seas and the sand,
    (Wi' sax leal maidens a' waiting my ca'.)

      " Auld uncle John wha wedlock's joys,
      Sioce *Mar's year* * did desire ;
      Because he gat the toom-dish thrice,
      He heaved them on the fire."

  * *Wi' death an' his sand-glass on the martyrs' stane.* The martyrs, as it is
well known, are those unfortunate people who perished in the deadly struggle of
the Church of Scotland with English prelacy. Their graves were marked out
by their countrymen with hewn stones (called the martyrs' stanes,) rudely sculp-
tured, and strewn with rhymes of scriptural denunciation against their perse-
cutors. The ground where they are interred is consecrated with devotional
pilgrimage.

           * *Mar's year*, 1715.
           N

Ye maun plow't a' wi' a braid elf-arrow,*
  (Far maun ye gang ere ye come to my ha'),
Ye maun rake out the weeds wi' a gowd-teethed
    harrow,
  (A hill o' heckle teeth for to climb owre an a'.)

Ye maun saw't a' wi' ae pyle o' corn,
  (Deil get the clungest quo the haggis to claw !)
That never had chaff on't since man was born,
  (The birds pair kindliest when they're nestlings
    an' a'.)

To wear aff the birds, be a *scaur-craw* yoursel,
  (The gled pykes the banes o' the auld hoodie
    craw.)
And there's never a corbie daur play pouk at yere
    tail,
  (The flowers spring up whan the spring winds
    blaw.)

Ye maun weet it wi' dew that never has fa'n,
  (There's a sour crab grows at our barn wa',)
Ye maun cool't a' wi' wind that never has blawn,
  (And the birds winna big in't nor sing in't ava.)

It mauna grow wi' its tap to the sun,
  (O love pairs low like blythe birds twa ;)
But maun streek up and ripen wi' the light o' the
    moon,
  (Ye may catch a young lass like a bird i' the snaw.)

---

* See the history of the fairies, Appendix (F.)

Ye maun shear't a' wi' a young tup's horn,
    (I winna grip wi' chaff like a bird i' the snaw,)
That never had woo on't since man was born,
    (Ye maun catch me wi' corn if ye catch me at a'.)

Ye maun thresh't out on yon castle tap,
    (The lintie chittles sad i' the high tower wa',)
And nae for yere life let ae pickle drap ;
    (The wee-bird's blythe whan the winter's awa.)

Ye maun sift it a' wi' a bottomless sieve,
    (The spring-gowan's cauld wi' it's happin of snaw,)
Ye maun sack it up, i' the thumb o' a glove,
    (But it keeks lovely out whan the sun 'gins to
        thaw.)

Ye maun kill-dry't wi' ice, ye maun grun't but a
    *quairn,**
    (Will ye big me a bowerique in simmer of snaw ;)
Ye maun barrel't i' the ring of an unchristen'd bairn,
    (The westlin star's comelie whan the sun sinks
        awa.)

---

* *Ye maun kill-dry't wi' ice, ye maun grun't but a quairn ;* little hand mills which are yet to be found in some old peoples' houses for grinding corn. They were common before water-mills became so general. These stones are thin and flat, made of field free-stone, and are called *quairns.* Besides these there were troughs found at every hamlet for the purpose of *knocking their bear in,* before barley mills were erected. Small kilns, with ribs of wood, covered with oat straw, over which was spread the corn, were the joint and common property of a few neighbours. Great care was taken while *beeting* the kiln lest they should fire the straw.
Thus the unfortunate Gudeman of Auchtermuchty,

      "Then he bore kendling to the kill,
      But scho start all up in a lowe,"

Ye maun make brydal brose o't but water or lowe,
(Twa todlin burns 'mang the birk banks fa')
Ye maun borrow smid-meal frae the fairie at the
knowe,
(I hae twa mills whilk the todlin burns ca'.)

Ye maun dish't a' out in a braid cockle-shell,
(Bride's maids are mim at a supper an' a',)
For my sax bride-maidens to sup at a meal,
(The gled lo'es gore, and the cat lo'es a'.)

And whan ye hae finish'd this bridegroom Darg,
(My white-sheeted bed is siller at the wa')
Come like a blythe wooster an' hansel yere Sark,
(An' there's armfu's o' love atween the sheets sma'.)

———

Not many of these songs appear to be very old; some
of them perhaps not above forty or fifty years. It may
be deemed proper to explain in what way they have
passed upon the breath of tradition. It is to the country-
meetings of men and women, young men and maidens,
that we owe their preservation, and often their rise. The
first kind of meeting that shall be noticed is the *Song
Trystes*. These were agreements of probably twenty or
thirty lads and lasses to meet at an appointed house,
(either a farmer's or a respectable cottar's,) for song-singing and merriment. There were also wool-combing and

spinning *Trystes*, which, though for the express purpose of friendly assistance, always ended and were mixed with singing songs and reciting ballads. These trysted themselves through part of a parish, until all the wool was carded and spun. Then were *Dancing Trystes*, which were twin sisters to those of song : the lads would carry wine and whiskey, with sweetmeats, to refresh their partners in the intervals of dancing. They then selected some of the most melting songs, such as were touched keenly with the finger of love ; these were sung by the young women, and their partners joined in the tenderest parts, which suited their own situations and feelings.

The *Lord's Marie* had its rise from one of these meetings, and it is a fine example of unadorned poesy, and of rustic taste. Many of the songs, however, were " higher-kilted " than is now meet for a modest ear. *Old Glenae*, a Nithsdale song, mentioned by Burns, in his " Remarks on Scottish Song," belongs to weddings and to dancing Trystes. It was sung in the character of an old man, worn down with age, and abounds with local humour, but it is too gross for insertion. It begins—

> " Silly, poor, auld Glenae,
> What ails the kirk at thee ? "

Beside all these, there were *Halloween meetings*, which, though dedicated solely to spells and charms, and casting cantraips, were intermingled with song-singing and ballad-reciting.

To them we may justly place some of the most exquisite productions of the rural muse of Caledonia. Burns speaks of these meetings and their purposes :—

" On fasten een we had a rockin*
To ca' the crack and weave our stockin ;
An there was muckle fun an' jokin,
Ye need na doubt ;
At length we had a hearty yokin
At *sang about.*"

—EPISTLE TO J. LAPRAIK.

Eager to outshine his fellow peasants each selected
the finest song for pathos and humour, which was either
printed or recited. They laid hold of their own emotions of heart and dressed them up in rhyme. Their
own adventures, or particular state of feeling and affection, furnished ample scope for poetic display. The
taste of their sweethearts was the critical tribunal to
which they appealed, where love and nature were judges,
and affixed their seal of approbation. They knew no
higher court of appeal, nor dreaded passing below the
saws and harrows-of-iron of classic criticism.

To these meetings we may assign the many variations
and additions which are found in the old songs, and of
which, in the present collection, there are a few pointed
out, and specimens preserved.

---

* " There is another custom here, commonly known in the language of the
country by the name of *rocking* ; that is, when neighbours visit one another in
pairs, or three or more in company, during the moonlight of winter or spring,
and spend the evening alternately in one another's houses. It is here noticed,
because the custom seems to have arisen when spinning on the *rock* or *distaff*
was in use, which therefore was carried along with the visitant to a neighbour's
house. The custom still prevails, though the rock is laid aside ; and when one
neighbour says to another, in the words of former days, ' I am coming over with
my rock,' he means no more than to tell him that he intends to spend an evening
with him." See the account of the Parish of Muirkirk, Statist. Acc. VII. 612,
613.

SONGS

OF

THE NITHSDALE AND GALLOWAY PEASANTRY.

CLASS III.—JACOBITICAL.

(1715, 1745.)

JACOBITE SONGS, 1715.

DERWENTWATER.

(A FRAGMENT.)

James Radcliff, Earl of Derwentwater, commanded part of the rebel forces in the Rebellion of 1715. After an ill-concerted irruption he was taken prisoner at Preston, in Lancashire. He is reported to have been a beautiful and noble-looking man. Smollet observes that "Derwentwater was an amiable youth—brave, open, generous, hospitable and humane. His fate drew tears from the spectators, and was a great misfortune to the country in which he lived. He gave bread to multitudes of people whom he employed on his estate;—the poor, the widow, and the orphan, rejoiced in his bounty."— (*Hist. of Eng.*, Vol X., p. 200.) This is an amiable character, and though smirched with the foulness of rebellion, smells sweetly of heaven. The Editor cannot find any tradition on which this ballad is founded; it is taken from the recitation of a young girl, in the parish of Kirk-bean, in Galloway. He has searched for it care-

O

fully through all the collections he could meet with, but it is not to be found. There are many local songs which, perhaps, never passed the bounds of a few parishes. Revived by casual recitation among the peasantry, they rarely rise into further notice. In the vulgar mind we frequently observe the strongly-marked rudiments of critical judgment. Thus the peasantry retain those noble touches of nature which are scattered among their songs and ballads, while the indifferent verses which encompass them, like dross from the pure ore, are rejected and forgotten. Hence the many gaps in the Scottish ballads, and often single verses of sterling merit where no further traces can be discovered.

DERWENTWATER.

(A FRAGMENT.)

O Derwentwater's a bonnie Lord,
   Fu' yellow is his hair,
And glenting is his hawking ee,
   Wi' kind love dwalling there.

Yestreen he came to our lord's yett,
   An' loud, loud cou'd he ca',*

Could he ca', a Scotticism.

" Rise up, rise up, for gude King James,
    An' buckle, and come awa."

Our ladie held by her gude lord,
    Wi' weel luve-locked hands ;
But when young Derwentwater came,
    She loosed the snawy bands.

An' when young Derwentwater kneel'd,
    " My gentle fair ladie,"
The tears gave way to the glow o' love,
    In our gude ladie's ee.
       *   *   *   *

" I will think me on this bonnie ring,
    And on this snawy hand,
When on the helmy ridge o' weir*
    Comes down my burly brand.

" And I will think on thae links o' gowd,
    Which ring thy bonnie blue een,
When I wipe awa the gore o' weir,
    An' owre my braid sword lean."

O never a word our ladie spake,
    As he press'd her snawy hand,
An' never a word our ladie spake,
    As her jimpy waist he spann'd ;
But " O ! my Derwentwater," she sigh'd,
    When his glowing lips she fand.

---

* *Weir*, war.

He has drapp'd frae his hand the tassel o' gowd,
　　Which knots his gude weir glove;
An' he has drapped a spark frae his een,
　　Which gars our ladie love.

" Come down, come down," our gude lord says,
　　Come down my fair ladie,—
O dinna, young lord Derwent stop,
　　The morning sun is hie."—

And high, high raise the morning sun,
　　Wi' front o' ruddie blude,
" Thy harlot front frae thy white curtain,
　　Betokens naething gude."
　　　　*　　　*　　　*　　　*

Our ladie look'd frae the turret-top,
　　As lang as she could see;
And every sigh for her gude lord,
　　For Derwent there were three.
　　　　*　　　*　　　*　　　*

LAMENT FOR THE LORD MAXWELL.

This potent and honourable name is eminent for its heroic attachment to fallen royalty.

The Maxwells distinguished themselves by desperate feats of valour in the cause of the lovely and unfortunate Mary. At the fatal field of Langside they composed part of those gallant spearmen who, unseconded by their flinching countrymen, bore the awful shock of encounter from the furious and veteran phalanx of the Regent. When all was irrecoverably lost, they threw themselves around their beloved Queen, and accomplished the memorable retreat to Dundrennan Abbey, in Galloway.

The Maxwells opposed her rash and misguided resolve of trusting her sister Elizabeth. Not daring to confide in the hope of the returning loyalty and regard of her countrymen, she threw herself in the arms of England, a royal and lovely supplicant, and alas! a victim. The valour of the Maxwells was again awakened in the cause of her martyred grandson. When the royal standard was raised, Charles numbered among the remains of unshaken loyalty, the Maxwells of Nithsdale. Charles's letter, requesting the aid of the Nithsdale veterans, is preserved in Terreagle's House, the seat of Constable Maxwell, Esq.

Good or bad report could not subdue determined loyalty : the sword was again drawn for exiled royalty beneath the standard of Mar—and the punishment due to the movers of such a premature and ill-conducted effort fell upon those who, contrary to their better judgments, upheld the sinking cause even in the front of ruin.   The Earl of Nithsdale was taken prisoner at Preston, in Lancashire—tried and sentenced to decapitation ;—but by the extraordinary ability and admirable dexterity of his Countess he escaped out of the Tower on the evening before his sentence was to be executed, and died at Rome Anno 1744.*

LAMENT FOR THE LORD MAXWELL.

MAKE mane, my ain Nithsdale, thy leaf's i' the fa',
The lealest o' thy bairns are a' drapping awa ;
The rose i' thy bonnet whilk flourished ay sae braw,
Is laigh wi' the mools since Lord Maxwell's awa.

O wae be 'mang ye Southron,† ye traitor lowns a',
Ye haud him ay down wha's back's at the wa',
I' the eerie field o' Preston yere swords ye wadna draw,
O he lies i' cauld iron wha wad swappit ye a'.

---

* An account of this escape will be found in the Appendix.
† *Southron*, an old name for the English.

O wae be to the hand whilk drew nae the glaive,
And cowed nae the rose frae the cap o' the brave,
To hae thri'en 'mang the Southron as Scotsmen ay thrave,
Or ta'en a bluidy niev'ou o' fame to the grave.

The glaive for my countrie I doughtna then wauld,
Or I'd cocked up my bonnet wi' the best o' the bauld,
The crousest sud been cowpit owre i' death's gory fauld,
Or the leal heart o' some i' the swaird sud been cauld.

Fu' aughty simmer shoots o' the forest hae I seen,
To the saddle laps in blude i' the battle hae I been ;
But I never kend o' dule till I kend it yestreen,
O that I were laid whare the sods are growing green !

I tint half my sel' whan my gude Lord I did tine,
A heart half sae brave a brade belt will never bin',
Nor the grassy sods e'er cover a bosom sae kin',
He's a drap o' dearest blude in this auld heart o' mine.

O merry was the lilting amang our ladies a',
They danced i' the parlour and sang i' the ha',
"O Charlie he's come owre an' he'll put the Whigs awa,"
But they canna dight their tears now sae fast do they fa'!

Our ladie dow do nought now but wipe ay her een,
Her heart's like to loup the gowd lace o' her gown,
She has busked on her gay cleeding an's aff for Lon'on
        town,
An' has wi' her a' the hearts o' the countrie roun'.

By the bud o' the leaf—by the rising o' the flower,
'Side the sang o' the birds whare some burn tottles owre,
I'll wander awa there an' big a wee bit bower,
For to keep my gray head frae the drap o' the shower.

An' ay I'll sit an' mane till my blude stops wi' eild,
For Nithsdale's bonnie lord, wha was bauldest o' the
          bauld,
O that I were wi' him in death's gory fauld,
O had I but the iron on, whilk hauds him sae cauld !

The feelings of his peasantry on hearing of his escape,
though roughly Scottish, are worthy of record.

THE LUSTY CARLIN.

" WHAT news to me, Carlin ?
    What news to me ?"
" Enough o' news," quo' the lusty Carlin,
    Best news that God can gie."

" Has the duke hanged himsel', Carlin?
    Has the duke hanged himsel' ?
    Or has he ta'en frae the tither Willie
    The hettest neuk o' hell."

" The duke's hale an' fier, Carle,
    The duke's hale an' fier,
    An' our ain Lord Nithsdale
    Will soon be 'mang us here."

" Brush me my coat, Carlin,
 Brush me my shoon,
 I'll awa an' meet Lord Nithsdale
 Whan he comes to our town."

" Alake-a-day," quo' the Carlin,
" Alake the day," quo' she,
" He's owre in France at Charlie's hand,
 Wi' only ae pennie."

" We'll sell a' our corn, Carlin,
 We'll sell a' our bear,
 An' we'll send to our ain Lord
 A' our sette gear !"*

Make the piper blaw, Carlin,
Make the piper blaw ;
An' make the lads an' lasses baith,
Their souple legs shaw.

We'll a' be glad, Carlin,
We'll a' be glad ;
An' play " *The Stuarts back again,*"
To put the Whigs mad !

---

* *Sette Gear*, money placed at interest.

P

KENMURE'S ON AN' AWA, WILLIE.

William, Viscount Kenmure, was beheaded during the rebellion of 1715. He was a devout member of the Protestant church; was much regretted; and his memory is still revered by the peasantry of Galloway and Nithsdale. "He was a virtuous young nobleman, calm, sensible, resolute, and resigned." He was ancestor of the present Hon. John Gordon, of Kenmure. He departed from Kenmure, with about two hundred horsemen into England, from whence he never returned.

Part of this heroic song is printed in Ritson's *Collection of Scottish Songs*. It has long been popular in the low parts of Scotland. This copy of it is printed from the recitation of Mrs. Copland. It differs considerably from Ritson's copy. Mrs. Copland had selected some of the best verses from those various copies which the peasantry have of every old ballad and song.

The redeemed verses are in brackets: they are evidently of the same age as the others, and, where tradition is uncertain, poetic merit must decide.

KENMURE'S ON AN' AWA.

KENMURE'S on an' awa, Willie,
  Kenmure's on an' awa ;—
An' Kenmure's lord is the bonniest lord,
  That ever Gallowa' saw.

Success to Kenmure's band, Willie,
  Success to Kenmure's band ;
There was never a heart that feared a Whig,
  E'er rade by Kenmure's land.

[There's a rose in Kenmure's cap, Willie,
  There a rose in Kenmure's cap,
He'll steep it red in ruddie hearts' blede,
  Afore the battle drap.]

For Kenmure's lads are men, Willie,
  For Kenmure's lads are men ;
Their hearts an' swords are mettle true,
  An' that their faes shall ken !

They'll live an' die wi' fame, Willie,
  They'll live an' die wi' fame,
And soon wi' soun' o' victorie,
  May Kenmure's lads come hame !

Here's Kenmure's health in wine, Willie,
  Here's Kenmure's health in wine !
There ne'er was a coward o' Kenmure's blude,
  Nor yet o' Gordon's line.

[He kissed his ladie's hand, Willie,
  He kissed his ladie's hand ;
But gane's his ladie-courtesie,
  Whan he draws his bluidie brand.]

His ladie's cheek was red, Willie,
  His ladie's cheek was red ;
Whan she saw his steely jupes put on,
  Which smelled o' deadly feud.]

Here's him that's far awa, Willie,
  Here's him that's far awa !
And here's the flower that I loe best,
  The rose that's like the snaw !*

---

* In the "History of the late Rebellion," (Dumfries, 1718) the author warmly espouses the Whig interest, and is continually inveighing on the cruelties practised by the Jacobites. Such an outrage on humanity, however, he can no where adduce, as that of which government was guilty in allowing their mob to insult the Lords Nithsdale, Derwentwater, Kenmure, and other captive noblemen, during their approach to London. We record it in his own words :
" The prisoners above-named (with many others) who had been appointed to be carried to London, arrived there on the ninth of December. They were brought as far as Highgate by Brigadier Panton, Lieutenant-Colonel of Lumley's regiment of horse, under a guard of an hundred of his troopers ; and were there received by Major-General Tatton at the head of a detachment of about three hundred foot guards, and one hundred and twenty horse-grenadier guards. Here every one of them had his arms tied with a cord coming across his back; and being thus pinioned, they were not allowed to hold the reins of the bridle ; but each had a foot-soldier leading his horse : and being ranged into four divisions, according to the four different prisons to which they were allotted, and each division placed between a party of the horse grenadiers and a platoon of the foot ; in this manner General Tatton set out from Highgate about noon, and proceeded to London through innumerable crowds of spectators, who all of them expressed their utmost detestation of their rebellious attempt, by upbraiding them with their crime, shouting them along in this disgraceful triumph, and incessantly crying out King George for ever ; *no warming-pan bastard !* the mobs in the meantime marched before them, beating on a *warming-pan*, while the General's drums beat a triumphant march. After this, the noblemen, and three or four others, were sent to the Tower; Mr. Forster, M'Intosh, and about seventy more to Newgate ; sixty to the Marshalsea ; and seventy-two to the Fleet."

THE WEE, WEE GERMAN LAIRDIE.

I.

WHA the deil hae we got for a King,
  But a wee, wee German lairdie!
An' whan we gade to bring him hame,
  He was delving in his kail-yairdie.
Sheughing kail an' laying leeks,
  *But** the hose and but the breeks,
Up his beggar duds he cleeks,
  The wee, wee German lairdie.

II.

An' he's clapt down in our gudeman's chair,
  The wee, wee German lairdie;
An' he's brought fouth o' foreign leeks,
  An' dibblet them in his yairdie.
He's pu'd the rose o' English lowns,
  An' brak the harp o' Irish clowns,
But our thristle will jag his thumbs,
  The wee, wee German lairdie.

III.

Come up amang the Highland hills,
  Thou wee, wee German lairdie;
An' see how Charlie's lang kail thrive,
  He dibblit in his yairdie.

---

* *But,* without.

An' if a stock ye daur to pu',
   Or haud the yoking of a pleugh,
We'll break yere sceptre o'er yere mou',
   Thou wee bit German lairdie !

IV.

Our hills are steep, our glens are deep,
   Nae fitting for a yairdie ;
An' our norlan' thristles winna pu',
   Thou wee, wee German lairdie !
An' we've the trenching blades o' wier,
   Wad lib ye o' yere German gear ;
An' pass ye 'neath the claymore's sheer,
   Thou feckless German lairdie !

———

There are several variations of this curious old song ; some of them the Editor has seen, and heard sung. The one here preserved, seems a little more modern ; the others were more homely and coarse in their manner. The first verse of one of them runs thus :

" Wha the deil hae we got for a king ?
   But a wee bit German lairdie ;
An' whan we gade to bring him hame,
   He was delving in his yairdie !
He threw his dibble owre the dyke,
   An' brint his wee bit spadie ;
An' swore wi' a' the English he could,
   He'd be nae mair a lairdie !"

There are others which merit preservation.

" He'll ride nae mair on strae sonks,
    For gawing his German hurdies ;
But he sits on our gude King's throne,
    Amang the English lairdies.
        *   *   *   *

Auld Scotland, thou'rt owre cauld a hole,
    For nursing siccan vermin ;
But the very dogs o' England's court
    Can bark an' howl in *German !*"

AWA, WHIGS, AWA !

This old song has long been a favourite among all classes, probably for its beautiful tune. The two first verses may be found in the *Scots Musical Museum*. Those annexed have never been printed, perhaps from their strong and direct severity. We may deem it a fair specimen of that bitter humour which has so long rankled in the bigotry of zeal and party-dispute.

It is from the recitation of Mrs. Copland.

AWA, Whigs, awa, awa, Whigs, awa,
  Ye're but a pack o' traitor lowns,
  Ye'll ne'er do good at a'.
Our thristles flourish'd fresh and fair,
  An' bonnie bloom'd our roses,
But Whigs cam like a frost in June,
  An' wither'd a' our posies.
    Awa, Whigs, awa.

Our sad decay in Kirk and State,
  Surpasses my descriving ;
The Whigs came 'mang us for a curse,
  An' we hae done wi' thriving.
    Awa, Whigs, awa.

A foreign Whiggish lown brought seeds
  In Scottish yird to cover,
But we'll pu' a' his dibbled leeks,
  An' pack him to Hanover.
    Awa, Whigs, awa.

The deil he heard the stoure o' tongues,
  An' ramping came amang us ;
But he pitied us sae wi' cursed Whigs,
  He turned an' wadna wrang us.
    Awa, Whigs, awa.

The deil sat grim amang the reek,
  Thrang bundling brunstane matches ;
An' croon'd 'mang the beuk-taking Whigs,
  Scraps of auld Calvin's catches !
Awa, Whigs, awa, awa, Whigs, awa,
Ye'll run me out o' wun spunks,
    Awa, Whigs, awa.

In the copy printed in the *Museum* there are two verses which bear evident marks of the hand of Burns.

" Our ancient crown's fa'n in the dust,
  Deil blind them wi' the stoure o't ;
And write their names in his black beuk,
  Wha gae the Whigs the power o't ?

Grim vengeance lang has ta'en a nap,
  But we may see him wauken ;
Gude help the day when royal heads
  Are hunted like a mauken !"*

---

* *A mauken*, a hare.

Q

THE HIGHLAND LADDIE.

The Highland Laddie seems to be the son of James
VII.   This song belongs to the Lowlands of Scotland,
as the expression " ayont the Forth," sufficiently certifies.
It is printed from the recitation of the young girl who
contributed " Derwentwater." She says, " This song is
very true.   An old Catholic woman used to sing it to
me, when I was a child, and attached to it many more
verses of an inferior nature, which I have endeavoured
to separate from the good, and thus give the song a fairer
shape."

PRINCELY is my luver's weed,
  Bonnie laddie, Highland laddie,
His veins are fu' o' princely blude,
  My bonnie Highland laddie.

The gay bonnet maun circle roun',
  Bonnie laddie, Highland laddie ;
The brows wad better fa' a crown,
  My bonnie Highland laddie.

There's a hand the sceptre bruiks,
  Bonnie laddie, Highland laddie ;
Better it fa's the shepherd's creuk,
  My bonnie Highland laddie.

There's a hand the braid-sword draws,
 Bonnie laddie, Highland laddie ;
The gowd sceptre it seemlier fa's,
 My bonnie Highland laddie.

He's the best piper i' the north,
 Bonnie laddie, Highland laddie ;
An' has dang a' ayont the Forth,
 My bonnie Highland laddie.

Soon at the Tweed he mints* to blaw
 Bonnie laddie, Highland laddie ;
Here's the lad ance far awa'!
 The bonnie Highland laddie !

There's nae a southron fiddler's hum,
 Bonnie laddie, Highland laddie ;
Can bide the war pipe's deadly strum,
 My bonnie Highland laddie.

An' he'll raise sic an eldritch drone,
 Bonnie laddie, Highland laddie ;
He'll wake the snorers round the throne,
 My bonnie Highland laddie.

And the targe an' braid sword's twang,
 Bonnie laddie, Highland laddie ;
To hastier march will gar them gang,
 My bonnie Highland laddie.

---

* Intends.

Till frae his daddie's chair he'll blaw,
   Bonnie laddie, Highland laddie ;
" Here's the lad ance far awa,"
   My bonnie Highland laddie.

There are many old fragments of songs to the tune, and
repetitions of " The Highland Laddie."   Some parts of
them are characteristic and lively :

    *   *   *   *

A' the lasses o' Dunkel',
   Bonnie laddie, Highland laddie ;
Brew gude ale for Charlie's sel',
   My bonnie Highland laddie.

The bonniest May* in Dundee,
   Bonnie laddie, Highland laddie ;
Made down the bed for young Charlie,
   The bonnie Highland laddie.†

---

* Maiden.

† The Editor has been informed by some intelligent Highlanders that they
have many admirable Jacobite songs " ayont the Forth," in the Erse language.

MERRIE MAY THE KEEL ROWE.

This is a popular bridal tune in Scotland ; and, like many other fragments of Scottish song, has the Jacobitical rose growing among its love sentiments. It seems to be the original of that pretty household song

"Weel may the boatie rowe."

———

I.

As I came down the Canno' gate,
   The Canno' gate, the Canno' gate,
As I came down the Canno' gate,
   I heard a lassie sing, O ;
"Merry may the keel rowe,
   The keel rowe, the keel rowe,
Merrie may the keel rowe,
   The ship that my love's in, O !

II.

My love has breath o' roses,
   O' roses, o' roses,
Wi' arms o' lilie posies,
   To fauld a lassie in, O.
Merrie may the keel rowe,
   The keel rowe, the keel rowe,
Merrie may the keel rowe,
   The ship that my love's in, O !

III.

My love he wears a bonnet,
  A bonnet, a bonnet,
A snawy rose upon it,
  A dimple on his chin, O ;
Merrie may the keel rowe,
  The keel rowe, the keel rowe,
Merrie may the keel rowe,
  The ship that my love's in, O !

SONG OF THE CHEVALIER.

"TO DAUNTON ME."

This old song is in the possession of Mrs. Copland.
There are several variations of it, all bearing the same
stamp of desperate resolution.   Burns preserved a copy
of it, which is published in his *Remarks on Scottish Song*.
There is a slight difference in the last verse.   It is no
easy matter to procure a copy of an old song which has
been little in print without finding many interpolated
verses.   There is a stray verse which seems to have formed no part of the original song, but to have been annexed since the fatal rebellion of 1745.   It runs thus :

> O I hae scarce to lay me on,
> Of kingly fields were ance my ain ;
> Wi' the moorcock on the mountain-bree,
> But hardship ne'er can daunton me.

Of the many variations the Editor has selected what
he deemed the best :

> Up came the gallant chief Lochiel,
> An' drew his glaive o' nut-brown-steel,
> Says " Charlie set your fit to me,
> An' shaw me wha will daunton thee !"

This is extremely characteristic of the noble Lochiel.

To daunton me an' me sae young,
An' gude king James's auldest son !
O that's the thing that ne'er can be,
For the man's unborn that will daunton me !

O set me ance on Scottish land,
An' gie me my braid-sword in my hand,
Wi' my blue bonnet aboon my bree,
An' shaw me the man that will daunton me.

It's nae the battle's deadlie stoure,
Nor friends pruived fause that'll gar me cower ;
But the reckless hand o' povertie,
O ! that alane can daunton me.

High was I born to kingly gear,
But a cuif* came in my cap to wear,
But wi' my braid sword I'll let him see
He's nae the man will daunton me.

---

* *Cuif*—a simpleton, a ninny.

"I started, muttering, blockhead coof."

BURNS.

JACOBITE SONGS, 1745.

CARLISLE YETTS.

(A FRAGMENT.)

This affecting old fragment is copied by Mrs. Copland, and transmitted for publication with the following remarks :—

" There are songs belonging to the history of private families which are cherished by them with all the fondness of traditionary attachment. They are preserved with a romantic affection, like the gore-crusted weapons of heroic achievement. Such perhaps is the song of ' Carlisle Yetts.' It was composed apparently in those afflicting times of murder and desolation, when so many heads of our bravest countrymen ' dripped bloodie' on the gate-spikes of Carlisle. It seems by the strong passion displayed in it, to have been written when the blood was yet unwashen from the destroyer's hand.

" I do not think it to have been the composition of a woman. The mild composure of the female heart would have shrunk back from such gory and harrowing delineation. I rather think it to have been written by some of the unfortunate adherents of the Prince, when lurking from wood to hill, amid all the horrors of proscription."

R

CARLISLE YETTS.

*   *   *   *

WHITE was the rose in his gay bonnet,
  As he faulded me in his broached plaidie ;
His hand whilk clasped the truth o' luve,
  O it was ay in battle readie !
His lang lang hair in yellow hanks,
  Waved o'er his cheeks sae sweet and ruddie ;
But now they wave o'er Carlisle yetts
  In dripping ringlets clotting bloodie.

My father's blood's in that flower-tap,
  My brother's in that hare-bell's blossom,
This white rose was steeped in my luve's blood,
  An' I'll ay wear it in my bosom.

*   *   *   *

III.

When I came first by merry Carlisle,
  Was ne'er a town sae sweetly seeming ;
The White Rose flaunted owre the wall,
  The thristled banners far were streaming !
When I came next by merry Carlisle,
  O sad, sad seemed the town an' eerie !
The auld, auld men came out an' wept,
  "O maiden come ye to seek yere dearie ?"

*   *   *   *

v.

There's ae drap o' blude atween my breasts,
  An' twa in my links o' hair sae yellow ;
The tane I'll ne'er wash, an' the tither ne'er kame,
  But I'll sit an' pray aneath the willow.
Wae, wae upon that cruel heart,
  Wae, wae upon that hand sae bloodie,
Which feasts in our richest Scottish blude,
  An' makes sae mony a doleful widow.

It is somewhat remarkable, that amid all the popular
bigotry of Scotland in behalf of the reigning Prince, there
are no songs in defence of his rights, nor in praise of
their deliverer, the Duke of Cumberland. The Caledonian Muse, with a romantic attachment, seems to
have taken the part of the royal exile, and to have
caught hold of the distresses and ruin which overpowered
her country. Whoever is versant in the national poetry
of Scotland will readily subscribe to this opinion. The
gallant, but unsuccessful attempt of the followers of the
Chevalier, powerfully interested even those who were adverse to his cause. The bravery and generosity displayed by these unfortunate men, will always be remembered
to the honour of their nation ; while the merciless conduct of their conqueror will be branded with infamy.
The national feeling was strongly roused, and the poets
partook of the common sympathy. The Editor does not
remember to have met with a more glowing picture of
the outrages committed at that time, than is contained
in the following passage in a letter from Allan Cunningham, to Mrs. Fletcher of Edinburgh. "I remember,"

says he, "a verse of a ballad which I composed, descriptive of the ravages committed in my devoted Scotland in 1745 : "

"The orphan-child weeps by the flame-bursting cottage,
    And prints its light footsteps in circles of gore :—
It lifts the blood-locks of the brown-cheeked peasant,
    And screams o'er his wounds, to thy echoes Benmore."*

There is a ballad already published in the *Scots Musical Museum*, entitled "Crookie Den," or "The Duke of Cumberland's descent into Hell." It is the sublime of humour.

"WERE ye e'er at Crookie Den ?
    Bonnie laddie, Highland laddie ;
Saw ye Willie and his men ?
    My bonnie laddie, Highland laddie !

They're our faes, wha brint an' slew,
    Bonnie laddie, Highland laddie ;
There at last they gat their due,
    My bonnie laddie, Highland laddie.

The hettest place was fill'd wi' twa,
    Bonnie laddie, Highland laddie ;
It was Willie and his papa,
    My bonnie laddie, Highland laddie.

* The name of a high hill in Perthshire.

The deil sat girning i' the neuk,
　　Bonnie laddie, Highland laddie ;
Breaking sticks to roast the Duke,
　　My bonnie laddie, Highland laddie.

The bluidy monster gied a yell,
　　Bonnie laddie, Highland laddie ;
An' loud the laugh gade round a' hell,
　　My bonnie laddie, Highland laddie."

———

Without entering at all into the discussion of political differences which have been set at rest for ever, it is impossible to regard the sanguinary and unrelenting persecutions which ensued after the victory of Culloden without feelings of horror and regret. We are not to be surprised, therefore, that the peasantry of Scotland, harassed and provoked by those cruel visitations, should give vent to the bitterness of their feelings, by consigning their oppressors to all the miseries which rustic fancy, inspired by revenge, could devise. The above ballad, though keenly satirical, is but a sketch compared with the one we now present to the reader, which we have selected, as containing, in many passages, a singular union of the ludicrous with the horrible, not unworthy of the genius and the humour of Burns.

CUMBERLAND AND MURRAY'S DESCENT INTO HELL.

I.

KEN ye whare cleekie* Murray's gane?
He's to dwall in his lang hame;
The beddle† clapt him on the doup,
" Hard I've earned my gray groat :
Lie thou there, and sleep thou soun',
God winna waken sic a lown ! "

II.

Whare's his gowd, and whare's his gain,
He rakit out 'neath Satan's wame?
He has nae what 'll pay his shot,
Nor caulk the keel o' Charon's boat.
Be there gowd whare he's to beek,
He'll rake it out o' brunstane-smeek.

III.

He's in a' Satan's frything pans,
Scouth'ring the blude frae aff his han's ;
He's washing them in brunstane lowe,
His kintra's blude it winna thowe !
The hettest soap-suds o' perdition
Canna out thae stains be washin'.

---

* Ready to take an advantage—inclined to circumvent.
† *The Beddle*, the grave-digger.

IV.

Ae devil roar'd till hearse and roupet,*
" He's pyking the gowd frae Satan's poupit ! "
Anither roar'd wi' eldritch yell,
" He's howking the key-stane out o' hell,
To damn us mair wi' God's day-light ! "—
And he douked i' the caudrons out o' sight.

v.

He stole auld Satan's brunstane leister,†
Till his waukit loofs were in a blister ;
He stole his Whig-spunks tipt wi' brunstane,
And stole his scalping whittle's set-stane,
And out of its red hot kist he stole
The very charter rights o' hell.

VI.

" Satan tent weel the pilfering villain,
He'll scrimp yere revenue by stealin' :
Th' infernal boots in which you stand in,
With which your worship tramps the damn'd in,
He'll wyle them aff your cloven cloots,
And wade through hell-fire i' yere boots."

---

* Hoarse, as with a cold.

† *Leister*, is a pronged iron instrument, somewhat resembling Neptune's Trident, used to strike fish, and here poetically transferred to Satan. Burns, humorously enough, has made this spear part of the paraphernalia of Death, in his celebrated Satire on Dr. Hornbook.

> " An awfu' scythe, out-owre ae shouther,
>   Clear-dangling hang ;
> A three-taed *leister* on the ither
>   Lay, large and lang."

VII.

Auld Satan cleekit him by the spaul',
And stappit him i' the dub o' hell ;—
The foulest fiend there doughtna bide him,
The damn'd they wadna fry beside him.
Till the bluidy duke came trysting hither,
An' the ae fat butcher fry'd the tither !

VIII.

Ae devil sat splitting brunstane-matches,
Ane roasting the Whigs like bakers' batches;
Ane wi' fat a Whig was basting,
Spent wi' frequent prayer an' fasting ;
A' ceas'd whan thae twin butchers roar'd,
And hell's grim hangman stapt an' glow'r'd !

IX.

" Fye ! gàr bake a pye in haste,
  Knead it of infernal paste,"
Quo' Satan :—and in his mitten'd hand,
He hynt up bluidie Cumberland,
An' whittlet him down like bow-kail castock,
And in his hettest furnace roasted.

X.

Now hell's black table-claith was spread,
The infernal grace was reverend said :

Yap* stood the hungry fiends a' o'er it,
Their grim jaws gaping to devour it ;
When Satan cried out, fit to scouner,†
" Owre rank o' judgments' sic a dinner."
*   *   *

---

* Yap, or yape.   Having a keen appetite for food.

† *To scouner*, to nauseate.

HAME, HAME, HAME.

This song is printed from a copy found in Burns'
Common Place Book, in the Editor's possession.   It has
long been popular in Galloway and Nithsdale, and has
many variations, of which this is the best.

I.

Hame, hame, hame, hame fain wad I be,
O hame, hame, hame, to my ain countrie !
When the flower is i' the bud and the leaf is on the tree,
The larks shall sing me hame in my ain countrie ;
Hame, hame, hame, hame fain wad I be,
O hame, hame, hame, to my ain countrie !

II.

The green leaf o' loyaltie's begun for to fa',
The bonnie white rose it is withering an' a' ;
But I'll water't wi' the blude of usurping tyrannie,
An' green it will grow in my ain countrie.
Hame, hame, hame, hame fain wad I be,
O hame, hame, hame, to my ain countrie !

III.

O there's naught frae ruin my country can save,
But the keys o' kind heaven to open the grave,

That a' the noble martyrs wha died for loyaltie,
May rise again and fight for their ain countrie.
Hame, hame, hame, hame fain wad I be,
O hame, hame, hame, to my ain countrie !

IV.

The great are now gane, a' wha ventured to save,
The new grass is springing on the tap o' their graves ;
But the sun thro' the mirk, blinks blythe in my ee,
" I'll shine on ye yet in yere ain countrie."
Hame, hame, hame, hame fain wad I be,
Hame, hame, hame, to my ain countrie !

———

It is a fact no less remarkable than gratifying, that no
language, ancient or modern, affords an equivalent term
for that concentration of domestic felicity and attachment which constitutes the meaning of our word HOME.
A writer, equally celebrated for her eloquence and her
knowledge of human nature, has noticed this peculiarity,
and her illustration of it is striking, and indeed sublime.

" C'est en vain qu'un Anglais se plait un moment aux mœurs etrangères ; son
cœur revient toujours aux premieres impressions de sa vie. Si vous interrogez
des Anglais voguant sur un vaisseau à l'extremité du monde, et que vous leur
demandiez ou ils vont ; ils vous repondront : chez nous—*home*, si c'est en Angle-
terre qu'ils retournent. Leur vœux, leur sentimens, à quelque distance qu'ils
soient de leur patrie, sont toujours tournés vers elle."—CORINNE, Tome 11., 210.

It is this same endearing call of HOME which vibrates
on every chord of a Scotchman's heart ; which cheers

him in absence from his native country, and sustains him through every vicissitude of toil and danger. The minstrelsy of Scotland has, perhaps, a greater power over the heart when repeated in a strange land ; for, as each song possesses some local allusion, it brings imagination to the aid of memory, and thus produces a charm to soothe the woes even of banishment itself.

THE WAES O' SCOTLAND.

(FROM MRS. COPLAND.)

WHAN I left thee, bonnie Scotland,
  Thou wert fair to see,
Fresh as a bonnie bride i' the morn
  Whan she maun wedded be !

Whan I came back to thee, Scotland,
  Upon a May-morn fair,
A bonnie lass sat at our town-en',
  Kaming her yellow hair.

" O hey ! O hey ! " sung the bonnie lass,
  " O hey ! an' wae's me !
There's joy to the Whigs, an' land to the Whigs,
  And nocht but wae to me !

" O hey ! O hey ! " sung the bonnie lass,
  " O hey ! an' wae's me !
There's siccan sorrow in Scotland,
  As een did never see.

" O hey ! O hey for my father auld !
  O hey ! for my mither dear !
An' my heart will burst for the bonnie lad
  Wha left me lanesome here ! "

I had na gane in my ain Scotland
  Mae miles than twa or three,
Whan I saw the head o' my ain father
  Coming up the gate to me.

" *A traitor's head !* " and " *a traitor's head !* "
  Loud bawled a bluidy lown ;
But I drew frae the sheath my glaive o' weir,
  An' strake the reaver * down.

I hied me hame to my father's ha',
  My dear auld mither to see ;
But she lay 'mang the black izles †
  Wi' the death-tear in her ee.

O wha has wrocht this bluidy wark ?
  Had I the reaver here,
I'd wash his sark in his ain heart blude,
  And gie't to his dame to wear !

---

* *Reaver*, one who is alternately the robber and the defender of his country;
—one who alike pillages friends and foes.   Such were the Highlanders' inroads
upon the Lowlanders.   Annandale, a district in Dumfriess-shire, was once the
resort whence such banditti issued.   The Johnstones and Jardines, now two of
the most respectable families in the district, were chieftains or leaders, by hereditary right.   A bloody and fatal rivalship existed between them and the Maxwells of Nithsdale : hence disastrous and desperate inroads almost wasted both
divisions.   Large vaults of stone were used for the security of the chieftains'
cattle.   One of these was lately taken down at Dalswinton, of immense strength,
with a ponderous iron-door, which the old men said " was to keep out the Annandale thieves."
  " Johnstone and Jardine ride thieves a'," has been affixed as a satirical motto
below the marauder-crests.   A spur, with wings, is the Johnstone's arms.
  † Unburnt embers.

I hadna gane frae my ain dear hame
   But twa short miles and three,
Till up came a captain o' the Whigs,
   Says, " *Traitor, bide ye me !* "

I grippit him by the belt sae braid,
   It birsted i' my hand,
But I threw him frae his weir-saddle
   An' drew my burlie brand.

" Shaw mercy on me," quo' the lown,
   An' low he knelt on knee ;
But by his thie was my father's glaive,
   Whilk gude King Brus did gie.

An' buckled roun' him was the broider'd belt*
   Whilk my mither's hands did weave,
My tears they mingled wi' his heart's blude,
   An' reeked upon my glaive.

---

* The classical reader may trace a resemblance of this incident with that which decided the fate of Turnus, after his combat with Æneas. But it would be equally as unfair to accuse the author of this affecting ballad on that account, as it would have been in Mr. Addison to ground a charge of plagiarism on his parallel of Chevy-Chase with the Æneid. The absurdity of detracting from the merit of the moderns, because their genius approximates to that of the ancients, has perhaps never been better ridiculed than in the following repartee of Burns. He was quoting a brilliant sentiment in an old Scotch song, with his accustomed warmth, to a pedantic schoolmaster, who coolly observed, "that it was very good,—but the thought was in Horace." "That may be," replied Burns, " but Horace stole it from the Scotchman, and be d——d to him !"

I wander a' night 'mang the lands I own'd,
  Whan a' folk are asleep,
And I lie oure my father and mither's grave,
  An hour or twa to weep !

O fatherless, and mitherless,
  Without a ha' or hame,
I maun wander through my dear Scotland,
  And bide a traitor's blame.

THE SUN'S BRIGHT IN FRANCE.

(FROM MISS MACARTNEY.)

After the battle of Culloden the wretched fugitives were driven among the woods and mountains of Scotland, where many perished with hunger and fatigue. Some took refuge in foreign countries; and there are many affecting fragments of song which seem to have been the composition of those exiles. As it was treason to sing them, the names of their authors were concealed beyond a possibility of discovery, and it is probably owing to this circumstance that they are now passed away and forgotten. The following gives a simple and touching picture of the feelings of an exile.

THE SUN'S BRIGHT IN FRANCE.

THE sun rises bright in France,
　　And fair sets he;
But he has tint the blythe blink he had
　　In my ain countrie.

T

It's nae my ain ruin
  That weets ay my ee,
But the dear Marie I left a-hin',
  Wi' sweet bairnies three.

Fu' bonnilie lowed my ain hearth,
  An' smiled my ain Marie ;
O, I've left a' my heart behind,
  In my ain countrie.

O, I am leal to high heaven,
  An' it 'll be leal to me,
An' there I'll meet ye a' soon,
  Frae my ain countrie !

THE LAMENTATION OF AN OLD MAN OVER THE RUIN OF HIS FAMILY.

(MRS. COPLAND.)

*   *   *

I HAD three sons, a' young, stout, and bauld,
An' they a' lie at ither's sides bluidie and cauld ;
I had a hame wi' a sweet wife there,
An' twa bonnie grand-bairns my smiling to share ;
I had a steer o' gude owsen to ca',
An' the bluidie Duke o' Cumberland's ruined them a'.
Revenge and despair ay by turns weet my ee,
The fa' o' the spoiler I lang for to see ;
Friendless I lie, and friendless I gang,
I've nane but kind heaven to tell o' my wrang !
" Thy auld arm," quo' heaven, " canna strike down the
        proud,
I will keep to mysel' the avenging thy blood."*

---

* There cannot be ascertained any particular place to which these songs relate ; nor do they, like many others, bear evidence for themselves. Being fragments, the verses of local authority are perhaps lost.

THE LOVELY LASS OF INVERNESS.

I.

THERE liv'd a lass in Inverness,
　　She was the pride of a' the town,
She was blythe as a lark on the flower-tap,
　　When frae the nest it's newly flown.
At kirk she wan the auld folks luve,
　　At dance she wan the ladses' een ;
She was the blythest ay o' the blythe,
　　At wooster-trystes or Halloween.

II.

As I came in by Inverness,
　　The simmer-sun was sinking down,
O there I saw the weel-faur'd lass,
　　And she was greeting* through the town.
The gray-haired men were a' i' the streets,
　　And auld dames crying, (sad to see!)
"The flower o' the lads o' Inverness,
　　Lie bludie on Culloden-lee !"

---

* Weeping aloud.

III.

She tore her haffet-links of gowd,
   And dighted ay her comely ee ;
" My father lies at bluidie Carlisle,
   At Preston sleep my brethren three !
I thought my heart could haud nae mair,
   Mae tears could never blin' my ee ;
But the fa' o' ane has burst my heart,
   A dearer ane there ne'er could be !

IV.

" He trysted me o' luve yestreen,
   Of love-tokens he gave me three ;
But he's faulded i' the arms o' gory weir,
   Oh ne'er again to think o' me !
The forest-flowers shall be my bed,
   My food shall be the wild berrie,
The fa' o' the leaf shall co'er me cauld,
   And wauken'd again I winna be.

V.

O weep, O weep, ye Scottish dames,
   Weep till ye blin' a mither's ee ;
Nae reeking ha' in fifty miles,
   But naked corses sad to see.
O spring is blythesome to the year,
   Trees sprout, flowers spring, and birds sing hie ;
But oh ! what spring can raise them up,
   Whose bluidie weir has sealed the ee ?

VI.

The hand o' God hung heavie here,
  And lightly touched foul tyrannie !
It strake the righteous to the ground,
  And lifted the destroyer hie.
" But there's a day," quo' my God in prayer,
  " Whan righteousness shall bear the gree ;
I'll rake the wicked low i' the dust,
  And wauken, in bliss, the gude man's ee !" *

---

* There have been still ruder, if not older words than these, of which all that remain, perhaps, are four lines which Burns has adopted, and which form the first half stanza of his exquisite verses on this interesting subject.

The lovely lass o' Inverness,
  Nae joy nor pleasure can she see ;
For een and morn, she cries, alas !
  And ay the saut tear blins her ee.
Drumossie Moor, Drumossie day,
  A waefu' day it was to me ;
For there I lost my father dear,
  My father dear and brethren three.

Their winding sheet the bluidy clay,
  Their graves are growing green to see ;
And by them lies the dearest lad
  That ever blest a woman's ee !
Now wae to thee, thou cruel lord,
  A bluidy man I trow thou be :
For mony a heart thou hast made sair,
  That ne'er did wrang to thine or thee !

THE YOUNG MAXWELL.

This ballad is founded on fact. A young gentleman of the family of Maxwell,—an honourable and potent name in Galloway and Nithsdale,—being an adherent of Charles, suffered in the general calamity of his friends.

After seeing his paternal house reduced to ashes ; his father killed in its defence ; his only sister dying with grief for her father, and three brothers slain, he assumed the habit of an old shepherd ; and in one of his excursions singled out one of the individual men who had ruined his family. After upbraiding him for his cruelty, he slew him in single combat.

The Editor has taken some pains to ascertain the field of this adventure, but without success. It has been, in all likelihood, on the skirts of Nithsdale or Galloway. These notices being known only to a few of the Stuarts' adherents, have all perished along with the fall of their cause.

WHARE gang ye, thou silly auld carle ?
  And what do ye carry there ?
I'm gaun to the hill-side, thou sodger gentleman,
  To shift my sheep their lair.

Ae stride or twa took the silly auld carle,
    An' a gude lang stride took he :
" I trow thou be a feck auld carle,
    Will ye shaw the way to me ?"

And he has gane wi' the silly auld carle,
    Adown by the green-wood side ;
" Light down, and gang, thou sodger gentleman,
    For here ye canna ride."

He drew the reins o' his bonnie gray steed,
    An' lightly down he sprang :
Of the comeliest scarlet was his weir coat,
    Whare the gowden tassels hang.

He has thrown aff his plaid, the silly auld carle,
    An' his bonnet frae 'boon his bree ;
An' wha was it but the young Maxwell !
    An' his gude brown sword drew he !

Thou killed my father, thou vile South'ron !
    An' ye killed my breth'ren three !
Whilk brake the heart o' my ae sister,
    I lov'd as the light o' my ee !

Draw out yere sword, thou vile South'ron !
    Red wat wi' blude o' my kin !
That sword it crapped the bonniest flower
    E'er lifted its head to the sun !

There's ae sad stroke for my dear auld father !
There's twa for my brethren three !
An' there's ane to thy heart, for my ae sister,
Wham I lov'd as the light o' my ee !

The admirers of Scottish rustic poetry, of which this song is a beautiful specimen, are again indebted to the enthusiasm and fine taste of Mrs. Copland for the recovery and contribution of these verses. There is a variation in the third stanza, which would have been adopted had it not been an interpolation. It expressly points to the scene of encounter.

" And gane he has wi' the sleeky auld carle,
Around the hill sae steep ;
Until they came to the auld castle
Which hings owre *Dee* sae deep."*

---

* The noble strength of character in this ballad is only equalled by the following affecting story :—

In the Rebellion of 1745, a party of Cumberland's dragoons was hurrying through Nithsdale in search of rebels. Hungry and fatigued they called at a lone widow's house, and demanded refreshments. Her son, a lad of sixteen, dressed them up *lang kale and butter*, and the good woman brought new milk, which she told them was all her stock. One of the party inquired, with seeming kindness, how she lived. " Indeed," quoth she, " the cow and the kale yard, wi' God's blessing's a' my *mailen.*" He arose, and with his sabre killed the cow, and destroyed all the kale. The poor woman was thrown upon the world, and died of a broken heart ; the disconsolate youth, her son, wandered away beyond the inquiry of friends, or the search of compassion. In the continental war, when the British army had gained a great and signal victory, the soldiery were making merry with wine, and recounting their exploits—A dragoon roared out, " I once starved a Scotch witch in Nithsdale—l killed her cow and destroyed her greens ; but," added he, " she could live for all that, on her God,

U

LASSIE, LIE NEAR ME.

LANG hae we parted been,
  Lassie, my dearie,
Now are we met again,
  Lassie, lie near me.
    Near me, near me,
    Lassie, lie near me ;
    Lang hast thou lain thy lane,
    Lassie, lie near me.

Frae dread Culloden's field,
  Bluidy and dreary,
Mourning my country's fate
  Lanely and wearie ;
    Wearie, wearie,
    Lanely and wearie,
    Become a sad banish'd wight,
    Far frae my dearie.

Loud, loud the wind did roar,
  Stormy and e'erie,
Far frae my native shore,
  Far frae my dearie ;

---

as she said !" "And don't you rue it," cried a young soldier, starting up,
" don't you rue it ?" " Rue what ?" said he, "rue aught like that !" " Then,
by my G—d," cried the youth, unsheathing bis sword, "that woman was my
mother ! draw, you brutal villain, draw." They fought ; the youth passed his
sword twice through the dragoon's body, and, while he turned him over in the
throes of death, exclaimed, " *had you rued it you should have only been punished by your God !*"

Near me, near me,
Dangers stood near me,
Now I've escaped them a',
Lassie, lie near me.

A' that I hae endured,
Lassie, my dearie,
Here in thine arms is cured,
Lassie, lie near me.
Near me, near me,
Lassie, lie near me ;
Lang hast thou lain thy lane,
Lassie, lie near me.*

---

* It has been suggested that this song would *look* better if it were printed *Wife, lie near me*, instead of *Lassie, lie near me*. Had not the Editor thought that these songs, in their present garb, were worthy of all acceptation, he certainly would not have brought them before the public. He is conscious that he cannot by any attempt at this sort of squeamish delicacy atone for presumption. Who would pardon even Dr. Johnson and his brother commentators, if, instead of illustrating, they had dared to garble the works of the immortal Shakspeare? A licence of this sort, if once assumed, would lead to mischiefs of incalculable extent ; every puny critic would be correcting and altering, until the original text of an author would no longer be known. What would then become of the standard works of our poets? Their finest effusions, their boldest flights, their most vivid descriptions, would be all at the mercy of those witlings, who fancy that the power of discovering faults implies the power of correcting them, and whose vanity in displaying that power is only equalled by their abuse of it.

It is hardly possible to fix a standard of public taste by which each poem might be tried and qualified for general approbation. The fable of the old man whose wives plucked his head bald because one disliked white hairs and the other black ones, shewed the futility as well as the danger of attending to these scruples. It would be easy to alter detached parts of these songs with some effect, but not without destroying the good old harmony of the whole. In fact, there appears to be no other way of *mending* the writings of these forgotten bards but as the Highlander mended his gun :—" He gave it a *new stock*, a *new lock*, and a *new barrel*."

BANNOCKS O' BARLEY.

In the *Scots Musical Museum* there is but one verse and a half preserved of this song. One is surprised and incensed to see so many fine songs shorn of their very best verses for fear they should exceed the bounds of a page ! The Editor has collected the two last heart-rousing verses, which, he believes, will complete the song.

BANNOCKS o' bear-meal, bannocks o' barley,
Here's to the Highlandman's bannocks o' barley !
Wha in a bruilzie * will first cry " a parley ! "
Never the lads wi' the bannocks o' barley !
    Bannocks o' bear-meal, bannocks o' barley,
    Here's to the Highlandman's bannocks o' barley !

Wha drew the gude claymore for Charlie ?
Wha cow'd the lowns o' England rarely ?
An' claw'd their backs at Falkirk fairly ?——
Wha but the lads wi' the bannocks o' barley !
    Bannocks o' bear-meal, &c.

---

* A scuffle, a quarrel.

Wha, when hope was blasted fairly,
Stood in ruin wi' bonnie Prince Charlie?
An' neath the Duke's bluidy paws dreed fu' sairly?
Wha but the lads wi' the bannocks o' barley!*
Bannocks o' bear-meal, &c.

---

* Among the brave supporters of Prince Charles, few excited greater admiration than the seven Highlanders who concealed him in *Glenmorriston's Cave*, and, in disguise, procured necessaries and information. Although fugitives, and in poverty, these seven had the nobleness of mind to prefer fidelity to the man whom they considered as their prince, to *thirty thousand pounds*, the reward offered for his person. (See Home's *History of the Rebellion*, if it be proper to call that a *history*, in which facts of the first importance are deliberately and dishonestly concealed, and in which the severities inflicted after the battle of Culloden are altogether omitted.) But of all the men who preserved an unshaken fidelity to the Chevalier in his falling fortunes, the most heroic was Roderick M'Kenzie, who sacrificed his life for him, with a presence of mind and a self-devotion unparalleled either in ancient or in modern story.

"About this time, one Roderick M'Kenzie, a merchant of Edinburgh, who had been out with the Prince, was skulking among the hills about Glenmorriston, when some of the soldiers met with him. As he was about the Prince's size and age, and not unlike him in the face, being a genteel man and well dressed, they took him for the Prince. M'Kenzie tried to escape them but could not, and being determined not to be taken and hanged (which he knew, if taken, would be his fate), he bravely resolved to die sword in hand; and, in that death, to serve the Prince more than he could do by living. The bravery and steadiness of M'Kenzie confirmed the soldiers in the belief *that he was the Prince*, whereupon one of them shot him; who, as he fell, cried out, 'You have killed your Prince, you have killed your Prince,' and expired immediately. The soldiers, overjoyed with their supposed good fortune in meeting with so great a prize, immediately cut off the brave young man's head, and made all the haste they could to Fort Augustus, to tell the news of their great heroical feat, and to lay claim to the thirty thousand pounds, producing the head, which several said they knew to be the Prince's head. This great news, with the head, was soon carried to the Duke, who, believing the *great work* was done, set forward to London from Fort Augustus on the eighteenth of July."

YOUNG AIRLY.

This beautiful fragment is evidently copied from an old song called " *The Bonnie House o' Airlie.*" Probably some proscribed minstrel of 1745 has infused into it the stronger poetic glow of Jacobitism. "Young Airlie" was eldest son to Ogilvie, Earl of Airlie, and with his father's vassals joined Prince Charles. He married a daughter of Johnstone of Westerhall in Annandale—a lady of characteristic· family courage, who followed her lord through all the dangers and troubles of war. In the hasty march through Dumfries, a confidential friend wished Lady Ogilvie to return to her father's from the uncertain tumult of rebellion. " O ! Mary (said she) Charlie's the righteous heir ! wha wadna gang wi' Charlie ! " Young Lord Airlie escaped to France after the battle of Culloden.

YOUNG AIRLY.

*   *   *   *

" Ken ye aught o' gude Lochiel,
  Or ken ye aught o' Airly ? "
" They've buckled them on their weir-harnessing,
  An' aff an' awa wi' Charlie."

" Bring here to me," quo' the hie Argyle,
  " My bands in the morning early,
  An' we'll raise sic a lowe that heaven shanna sloken
    In the dwalling o' young Lord Airly ! "

" What lowe is yon?" quo' the gude Lochiel,
  " Whilk rises wi' the sun sae early?"
" By the God o' my kin," quo' the young Ogilvie,
  " It's my ain bonnie hame o' Airly ! "

" Put up yere sword," quo' the gude Lochiel,
    An' " put it up," quo' Charlie,
" We'll raise sic a lowe roun' the fause Argyle !
    An' light it wi' a spunk frae Airly."

It's nae my ha', nor my lands a' reft,
  Whilk reddens my cheeks sae sairlie ;
But my mither an' twa sweet babies I left
  To smoor i' the reek o' Airly."

THE HIGHLAND WIDOW'S LAMENT.

This song has been known in another garb, for many years in Galloway. The three last verses, within brackets, are now first printed. The fifth, sixth, and seventh verses are wholly by BURNS. He sent a copy of it to the *Scots Musical Museum.*

———

O ! I am come to the low countrie,
   Ochon, ochon, ochrie !
Without a penny in my purse
   To buy a meal to me.

It was nae sae in the Highland hills,
   Ochon, ochon, ochrie !
Nae woman in the country wide
   Sae happy was as me.

For then I had a score o' kye,
   Ochon, ochon, ochrie !
Feeding on yon hill sae high,
   And giving milk to me.

And there I had three-score o' yowes,
   Ochon, ochon, ochrie !
Skipping on yon bonnie knowes,
   And casting woo to me.

I was the happiest of a' the clan,
  Sair, sair may I repine,
For Donald was the bravest man,
  And Donald he was mine !

Till Charlie Stewart cam at last
  Sae far to set us free ;
My Donald's arm was wanted then,
  For Scotland and for me.

Their waefu' fate what need I tell !
  Right to the wrang did yield ;
My Donald and his country fell
  Upon Culloden field !

[I hae nocht left me ava,
  Ochon, ochon, ochrie !
But bonnie orphan lad-weans twa,
  To seek their bread wi' me.

[I hae yet a tocher band,
  Ochon, ochon, ochrie !
My winsome Donald's durk an' bran', ⅂
  Into their hands to gie—
                  W

[There's only ae blink o' hope left,
   To lighten my auld ee,
To see my bairns gie bludie crowns *
   To them gar't Donald die ! †]

---

* *Crowns,* or *Crouns*—the skull, or crown of the head.

"Clowr'd snouts, an' bluidie crowns,"

OLD SCOTTISH BALLAD.

† The determined fierceness of the Highland character urges to acts of desperate resolution and heroism. One of a clan, at the battle of Culloden, being singled out and wounded, set his back against a park wall, and with his targe and claymore bore singly the onset of a party of dragoons. Pushed to desperation, he made resistless strokes at his enemies, who crowded and encumbered themselves to have each the glory of slaying him. "Save that brave fellow," was the unregarded cry of some officers. *Golice Macbane* was cut to pieces, and thirteen of his enemies lay dead around him.

CHARLIE STEWART.

The following affecting heroic verse concludes all the Jacobite songs of merit that could be collected.*

---

*   *   *   *

O DREARY laneliness is now
   'Mang ruin'd hamlets smoking,
Yet the new-made widow sits an' sings
   While her sweet babe she's rocking :
" On DARIEN think, on dowie GLENCOE,
   On MURRAY, traitor coward !
On CUMBERLAND's blood-blushing hands,
   And think on CHARLIE STEWART ! "

---

* These songs, with the exception of one or two pieces, have been taken down from recitation chiefly of Catholic families, in Nithsdale and Galloway, by whom they were preserved and communicated with an enthusiasm proportioned to their attachment to the cause. The reader may refer to Ritson's two volumes of Scottish Songs and Ballads, in which he will find a selection of Jacobite songs from copies already printed, which, the Editor conceives, will nearly complete the collection.

SONGS

OF

THE NITHSDALE AND GALLOWAY PEASANTRY.

CLASS IV.—OLD BALLADS AND FRAGMENTS.

OLD BALLADS AND FRAGMENTS.

WE WERE SISTERS, WE WERE SEVEN.

This curious legend is one among a considerable number which were copied from the recital of a peasant-woman of Galloway, upwards of ninety years of age. They were all evidently productions of a very remote date, and, whatever might be their poetical beauties, were so involved in obscurity as to render any attempt at illustration useless. This tale was preserved as a specimen of the rest, being not only the clearest in point of style, but possessing a character of originality which cannot fail to interest the reader. Though not strictly what may be called a fairy tale, it is narrated in a similar way. The transitions are abrupt, yet artfully managed, so as to omit no circumstance of the story which the imagination of the reader may not naturally supply. The singular character of Billie Blin' (the Scotch Brownie, and the lubbar fiend of Milton) gives the whole an air of the marvellous, independently of the mystic chair, on which the principal catastrophe of the story turns.

In the third volume of Mr. Scott's *Border Minstrelsy* there is a ballad called " Cospatrick," founded on three more imperfect readings of this ancient fragment, interspersed with some patches of modern imitation. The entire piece is not so long as the present copy, and the supplementary part but ill accords with the rude simplicity of the original. It is like the introduction of modern masonry to supply the dilapidations of a Gothic ruin ; the style of architecture is uniform, but the freshness and polish of the materials destroy the effect of the ancient structure, and it can no longer be contemplated as a genuine relique of past ages.

There are many incongruities in Mr. Scott's copy, which it is strange that so able an antiquary could have let pass.   For example :—

> " When bells were rung, and mass was said,
>   And a' men unto bed were gane."

In the Romish service we never heard of mass being said in the evening, but vespers, as in the original here given. Mr. Scott also omits that interesting personage the " Billie Blin," and awkwardly supplies the loss by making the bed, blanket, and sheets speak, which is an outrage on the consistency even of a fairy tale.

WE WERE SISTERS, WE WERE SEVEN.

WE were sisters, we were seven,
We were the fairest under heaven,
And it was a' our seven-years' wark
'To sew our father's seven sarks ;
And whan our seven years' wark was done
We laid it out upo' the green :
We coost the lotties * us amang
Wha wad to the greenwood gang,
To pu' the lily but and the rose
To strew witha' our sisters' bowers.
I was youngest, my weer was hardest,
And to the green-wood I bud† gae,
There I met a handsome childe,
High-coled stockings and laigh-coled shoon,
He bore him like a king's son ;
An' was I weel or was I wae,
He keepit me a' the simmer-day,
An' though I for my hame gaun sich,
He keepit me a' the simmer-night ; ·
He gae to me a gay gold ring,
And bade me keep it aboon a' thing.
He gae to me a cuttie knife,
And bade me keep it as my life.
Three lauchters o' his yellow hair,
For fear we wad ne'er meet mair.

     *   *   *

---

  * Lots.   † Must.

     X

First blew the sweet, the simmer-wind,
Then autumn wi' her breath sae kind,
Before that e'er the guid knight came
The tokens of his luve to claim.
Then fell the brown an' yellow leaf
Afore the knight o' luve shawed prief;
Three morns the winter's rime did fa',
When loud at our yett my luve did ca'—
"Ye hae daughters, ye hae seven,
Ye hae the fairest under heaven;
I am the lord o' lands wide,
Ane o' them maun be my bride—
I am lord of a' baronie,
Ane o' them maun lie wi' me—
O cherry lips are sweet to pree,
A rosie cheek's meet for the ee;
Lang brown locks a heart can bind,
Bonny black een in luve are kind;
Sma' white arms for clasping's meet,
Whan laid atween the bridal-sheets;
A kindlie heart is best of a',
An' debonnairest in the ha'.
Ane by ane thae things are sweet,
Ane by ane in luve they're meet—
But when they a' in ae maid bide,
She is fittest for a bride—
Sae be it weel or be it wae,
The youngest maun be my ladie;
Sae be it gude, sae be it meet,
She maun warm my bridal-sheet.

Little ken'd he, whan aff he rode,

I was his token'd luve in the wood ;
Or when he gied me the wedding-token,
He was sealing the vows he thought were broken.
First came a page on a milk-white steed,
Wi' golden trappings on his head,
A' gowden was the saddle lap,   .
And gowden was the page's cap ;
Next there came shippes three,
To carry a' my bridal-fee——
Gowd were the beaks, the sails were silk,
Wrought wi' maids' hands like milk ;
They came toom and light to me,
But heavie went they waie frae me.
They were fu' o' baken bread,
They were fu' of wine sae red—
My dowry went a' by the sea,
But I gaed by the greenwode tree ;
An' I sighed and made great mane,
As thro' the greenwode we rade our lane ;
An' I ay siched an' wiped my ee,
That e'er the greenwode I did see——
" Is there water in your glove,
   Or win' into your shoe ?
   O am I o'er low a foot-page,
   To rin by you ladie ! "
" O there's nae water in my glove,
   Nor win' into my shoes,
   But I am maning for my mither,
   Wha's far awa frae me."
               *   *   *
" Gin ye be a maiden fair,
   Meikle gude ye will get there,

If ye be a maiden but,*
Meikle sorrow will ye get ;—
For seven kings' daughters he hath wedded,
But never wi' ane o' them has bedded ;
He cuts the breast frae their breast-bane,
An' sends them back unto their dame.
He sets their back unto the saddle,
An' sends them back unto their father :
But be ye maiden or be ye nane,
To the gowden chair ye draw right soon ;
But be ye leman or be ye maiden,
Sit nae down till ye be bidden."

Was she maiden, or was she nane,
To the gowden chair she drew right soon,
Was she leman, or was she maiden,
She sat down ere she was bidden.

Out then spake the Lord's mother,
Says, "This is not a maiden fair ;
In that chair nae leal maiden
E'er sits down till they be bidden."
The *Billie Blin'*† then outspake he,
   As he stood by the fair ladie ;
"The bonnie May is tired wi' riding,
   Gaur'd her sit down ere she was bidden."
           *   *   *
But on her waiting-maid she ca'd,
" Fair ladie, what's your will wi' me?"

---

* *i. e.* If you are not a maid.   † See Appendix.

O ye maun gie yere maidenheid,
This night to an unco' lord for me.
" I hae been east, I hae been west,
I hae been far beyond the sea,
But ay by greenwode, or by bower,
I hae keepit my virginitie.
But will it for my ladie plead,
I'll gie't this night to an unco lord."
  *   *   *

When bells were rung, an' vespers sung,
An' men in sleep were locked soun',
Childe Branton and the waiting maid
Into the bridal bed were laid.
O lie thee down, my fair ladie,
Here are a' things meet for thee ;
Here's a bolster for yere head,
Here is sheets an' comelie weids.
  *   *   *

" Now tell to me, ye Billie Blin',
If this fair dame be a leal maiden ? "
" I wat she is as leal a wight
As the moon shines on in a simmer-night ;
I wat she is as leal a May,
As the sun shines on in a simmer-day.
But your bonnie bride's in her bower,
Dreeing the mither's trying hour."
Then out o' his bridal bed he sprang,
An' into his mither's bower he ran :
" O mither kind, O mither dear,
This is nae a maiden fair ;
The maiden I took to my bride,
Has a bairn atween her sides.

The maiden I took to my bower,
Is dreeing the mither's trying hour."

Then to the chamber his mother flew,
And to the wa' the door she threw ;
She stapt at neither bolt nor ban',
Till to that ladie's bed she wan.
Says, " Ladie fair, sae meek an' mild,
Wha is the father o' yere child ? "
" O mither dear," said that ladie,
" I canna tell gif I sud die,
We were sisters, we were seven,
We were the fairest under heaven ;
And it was a' our seven years' wark,
To sew our father's seven sarks.
And whan our seven years' wark was done
We laid it out upon the green.
We coost the lotties us amang,
Wha wad to the greenwode gang ;
To pu' the lily but an' the rose,
To strew witha' our sisters' bowers.
I was youngest, my weer was hardest,
And to the greenwode I bu* gae.
There I met a' handsome childe
Wi' laigh-coled stockings and high-coled shoon,
He seemed to be some king's son ;
And was I weel or was I wae,
He keepit me a' the simmer-day ;
Though for my hame gaun I oft sicht,
He keepit me a' the simmer-night ;

---

* Must.

He gae to me a gay gold-ring,
An' bade me keep it aboon a' thing;
Three lauchters o' his yellow hair,
For fear that we suld ne'er meet mair.
O mither, if ye'll believe nae me,
Break up the coffer an' there ye'll see."
An ay she coost an ay she flang,
Till her ain gowd-ring came in her hand;
And scarce aught i' the coffer she left,
Till she gat the knife wi' the siller-heft;
Three lauchters o' his yellow hair,
Knotted wi' ribbons dink and rare:
She cried to her son "whare is the ring
Your father gave me at our wooing,
An' I gae you at your hunting?
What did ye wi' the cuttie-knife,
I bade ye keep it as yere life?"
"O haud yere tongue, my mither dear,
I gae them to a lady fair;
I wad gie a' my lands and rents,
I had that ladie within my brents;
I wad gie a' my lands an' towers,
I had that ladie within my bowers."
"Keep still yere lands, keep still yere rents,
Ye hae that ladie within yere brents;
Keep still yere lands, keep still yere towers,
Ye hae that lady within your bowers."

Then to his ladie fast ran he,
An' low he kneeled on his knee;
"O tauk ye up my son," said he,
"An', mither, tent my fair ladie;

O wash him purely i' the milk,
And lay him saftly in the silk ;
An' ye maun bed her very soft,
For I maun kiss her wondrous oft."

It was weel written on his breast bane,
Childe Branton was the father's name ;
It was weel written on his right hand,
He was the heir o' his daddie's land.

TWO VERSES OF LOGAN BRAES.

(FROM MRS. COPLAND.)

IT was nae for want, it was nae for wae,
That he left me on the Logan brae :
There was lint in the dub, and maut in the mill,
There was bear in the trough and corn in the kill.

*   *   *

The wind it was lowne, the larks had left the sky,
The bats were a' flown, the herds had left the kye ;
The sheep were a' faulded, nought was muvin but the
      moon,
As we wander'd through the rye to the lang yellow
      broom.

O WHO IS THIS UNDER MY WINDOW?

This old song is taken down from the singing of Martha Crosbie, from whose recitation Burns wrote down the song of " The Waukrife Minnie.''

It has a fine affecting tune, and is much sung by the young girls of Nithsdale.   Burns has certainly imitated the last verse of it in his " Red, red Rose."

" O who is this under my window ?
O who is this that troubles me ? "
" O it is ane wha is broken-hearted,
Complaining to his God o' thee."

" O ask your heart, my bonnie Mary,
O ask your heart gif it minds o' me !"
" Ye were a drap o' the dearest bluid in't,
Sae lang as ye were true to me."

" If e'er the moon saw ye in my arms, love,
If e'er the light dawned in my ee,
I hae been doubly fause to heaven,
But ne'er ae moment fause to thee.

" My father ca'd me to his chamber,
Wi' lowin' anger in his ee ;
Gae put that traitor frae thy bosom,
Or never mair set thy ee on me.

" I hae wooed lang love—I hae loved kin' love,
 An' monie a peril I've braved for thee ;
I've traitor been to monie a ane love,
 But ne'er a traitor nor fause to thee.

" My mither sits hie in her chamber,
 Wi' saute tears happin' frae her ee ;
O he wha turns his back on heaven,
 O he maun ay be fause to thee ! "

" Gang up, sweet May, to thy ladie mother,
 An' dight the saute tears frae her ee ;
Tell her I've turned my face to heaven,
 Ye hae been heaven owre lang to me ! "

O up she rose, and away she goes,
 Into her true love's arms to fa' ;
But ere the bolts and the bars she loosed,
 Her true love was fled awa.

" O whare's he gane whom I lo'e best,
 And has left me here for to sigh an' mane ;
O I will search the hale world over,
 'Till my true love I find again.

" The seas shall grow wi' harvests yellow,
 The mountains melt down wi' the sun ;
The labouring man shall forget his labour,
 The blackbird shall not sing but mourn,
If ever I prove fause to my love,
 Till once I see if he return."

LADY MARGERIE.

With the exception of a few unconnected fragments, nothing now remains of this old ballad. The reader, however, may be pleased to peruse the legend as recorded by the traditions of Galloway.

Lady Margerie, the heroine of the song, was beloved by two brothers, sons of a neighbouring Baron. The suit of the youngest, whose name was Henry, being rejected, he, by ingeniously imitating his brother's writing, obtained an interview in an adjacent wood, and warmly brought his fair one to regard his tenderness with less indifference. The language of the youth in this instance, though homely, is pathetically expressive :

> " D' ye mind, d' ye mind, Lady Margerie,
>   When we handed round the beer :
> Seven times I fainted for your sake,
>   And you never dropt a tear.
>
> D' ye mind, d' ye mind, Lady Margerie,
>   When we handed round the wine ;
> Seven times I fainted for your sake,
>   And you never fainted once for mine."

She expostulated with him on the impropriety of bringing her into an unfrequented place for the purpose of winning affections, which, she observed, were not hers to bestow. But finding him determined to have either a favourable answer or a peremptory refusal, she frankly confessed that she was with child by his brother. Frantic at the loss of all he loved and valued, the young man drew his sword, and, with the characteristic barbarity of those rude times, cruelly murdered the lady.

The following stanza presents an image too horrible to be contemplated, were it not immediately coupled with a wildly sublime thought :

> " And he's ta'en the baby out of her womb,
> And thrown it upon a thorn :
> Let the wind blow east, let the wind blow west,
> The cradle will rock its lone."

The horrid deed was no sooner done, than the elder brother was apprised of it as he pursued the boar in a neighbouring forest ; for it would seem that supernatural agency was more frequent in those times than at present. The young hunter was following his game with ardour, cheering his dogs and poising his lance, ready to engage the monster when at bay :

> " But when brother Henry's cruel brand
> Had done the bloody deed,
> The silver-buttons flew off his coat,
> And his nose began to bleed."*

Astonished at this singular phenomenon, he immediately flew to the bower of his mistress, where a page in-

---

* The circumstances mentioned in the two last lines of this verse are believed by the vulgar in Scotland to be preternatural signs to announce the commission of murder.

formed him she was gone to the " silver wood," agreeably to his desire.   Thither he spurred his horse, and meeting Henry with his bloody sword still in his hand, inquired what he had been killing.   The other replied :—

> " O 1 have been killing in the silver wood
>   What will breed mickle woe ;
>   O 1 have been killing in the silver wood
>   A dawdy and a doe."

A mutual explanation took place, and Henry fell by the sword of his unhappy brother.   How much truth may be in this legend is uncertain, time having so thoroughly effaced every vestige of the supposed savage transaction, that even the finger of tradition points not to the place where the tragedy was acted.   Some of the old people of Galloway still retain the thread of the story, with the few wild detached stanzas here presented to the reader.

YOUNG AIRLY.

There are several copies of this Song, one of which begins thus—

"The great Argyle raised ten thousand men
    E'er the sun was waukening earlie ;
And he marched them down by the back o' Dunkel',
    Bade them fire on the bonnie house o' Airlie."

The following appears to be an older copy, and has finer touches of poetic merit.

IT fell in about the Martinmas time,
    An' the leaves were fa'ing early,
That great Argyle an' a' his men came
    To plunder the bonnie House o' Airly.

"Come down and kiss me, Ladie Ogilvie,
    Come down an' kiss me early ;
Come down an' kiss me, Ladie Ogilvie,
    Or there's be nae a stanning stane o' Airly."

" I winna kiss thee, great Argyle,
    At night or morning early ;
I winna kiss thee, thou fause, fause lord,
    If there should na be a stanning stane o' Airly.

But take me by the milk white hand,
 An' lead me down right hoolie ;
An' set me in a dowie, dowie glen,
 That I mauna see the fall o' Airly."—

He has ta'en her by the shouther blade,
 An' thurst her down afore him,
Syne set her upon a bonnie knowe tap,
 Bad her look at Airly fa'ing.

*   *   *

" Haste ! bring to me a cup o' gude wine,
 As red as ony cherrie ;
I'll tauk the cup, an' sip it up,
 Here's a health to bonnie Prince Charlie !

I hae born me eleven braw sons,
 The youngest ne'er saw his daddie ;
An' if I had to bear them a' again,
 They should a' gang alang wi' Charlie !

But if my gude Lord were here this night,
 As he's awa wi' Charlie ;
The great Argyle and a' his men,
 Durst na enter the bonnie House o' Airly.

Were my gude lord but here this day,
 As he's awa wi' Charlie ;
The dearest blude o' a' thy kin',
 Wad sloken the lowe o' Airly.

THE MERMAID OF GALLOWAY.

Tradition is yet rich with the fame of this bewitching Mermaid ; and many of the good old folks have held most edifying and instructing communion with her by her favourite moonlight banks and eddyed nooks of streams. She was wont to treasure their minds with her celestial knowledge of household economy, and would give receipts to make heavenly salve to heal the untimely touch of disease. A charming young girl, whom consumption had brought to the brink of the grave, was lamented by her lover. In a vein of renovating sweetness the good Mermaid sung to him—

" Wad ye let the bonnie May die i' yere hand,
An' the mugwort flowering i' the land."

He cropped and pressed the flower tops, and administered the juice to his fair mistress, who arose and blessed her bestower for the return of health.

The Mermaid's favourite haunts and couches were along the shores of the Nith and Orr, and on the edge of the Solway sea, which adjoins the mouths of those waters. Her beauty was such that man could not behold her face, but his heart was fired with unquenchable love. "Her long hair of burning gold," through the wiling links of which appeared her white bosom and

z

shoulders, were her favourite care; and she is always represented by tradition with one hand shedding her locks, and with the other combing them.

Tradition tells, that this world is an outer husk or shell, which encloses a kernel of most rare abode, where dwell the Mermaids of popular belief. According to Lowland mythology, they are a race of goddesses, corrupted with earthly passions—their visits to the world "though few and far between," are spoken of and remembered with awe—their affections were bestowed on men of exalted virtue and rare endowments of person and parts. They wooed in such a strain of syren eloquence that all hearts were fettered by the witcheries of love. When their celestial voice dropt on the ear, every other faculty was enthralled. They caught the beloved object in their embrace, and laid him on a couch, where mortal eyes might search in vain into the rites of such romantic and mysterious wedlock.

Though possessed of the most soft and gracious qualities, yet when a serious premeditated indignity was offered them, they were immediately awakened to revenge. A devout farm dame, in the time of the last persecution, was troubled in spirit at the wonted return of this heathenish visitant. A deep and beautiful pool, formed in the mouth of Dalbeattie burn, by the eddy of Orr Water, was a beloved residence of the Mermaid of Galloway. " I' the first come o' the moon " she would seat herself on a smooth block of granite, on the brink of the pool, comb her golden links of hair, and deliver her healing oracles.   The good woman, in a frenzy of religious zeal, with her Bible in her hand, had the temerity to tumble this ancient chair into the bottom of the pool.   The next morning her only child was found dead in its cradle, and a voice from the pool was often heard at day-close, by the distracted mother :

> " Ye may look i' yere toom cradle,
> And I'll look to my stane ;
> And meikle we'll think, and meikle we'll look,
> But words we'll ne'er hae nane ! "

All the noxious weeds and filth that could be collected, were thrown into the pool until the stream was polluted, and the Mermaid departed, leaving a curse of barrenness on the house, which all the neighbours for several miles around, are ready to certify has been faithfully fulfilled.

William Maxwell, Esq. of Cowehill, is the bridegroom " Willie " of this romance.   According to popular history, he was nephew to the " Lily of Nithsdale," heroine of the sublime song, " She's gane to dwall in Heaven."

Cowehill is beautifully situated on the banks of the river Nith, five miles above Dumfries, surrounded with groves of oak, and plantation trees, and is now the seat of —— Johnstone, Esq.

THE MERMAID OF GALLOWAY.

(FROM TRADITION.)

THERE's a maid has sat o' the green merse side
  Thae ten lang years and mair;
An' every first night o' the new moon
  She kames her yellow hair.

An' ay while she sheds the yellow burning gowd,
  Fu' sweet she sings an' hie,
Till the fairest bird that wooes the green wood,
  Is charm'd wi' her melodie.

But wha e'er listens to that sweet sang,
  Or gangs the fair dame te;*
Ne'er hears the sang o' the lark again,
  Nor waukens an earthlie ee.

It fell in about the sweet simmer month,
  I' the first come o' the moon,
That she sat o' the tap of a sea-weed rock,
  A-kaming her silk-locks down.

Her kame was o' the whitely pearl,
  Her hand like new-won milk;
Her breasts were a' o' the snawy curd,
  In a net o' sea-green silk.

---

* To.

She kamed her locks owre her white shoulders,
   A fleece baith bonny and lang ;
An' ilka ringlet she shed frae her brows,
   She raised a lightsome sang.

I' the very first lilt o' that sweet sang,
   The birds forhood* their young ;
An' they flew i' the gate o' the gray howlet,
   To listen the sweet maiden.

I' the second lilt o' that sweet sang,
   Of sweetness it was sae fu' ;
The tod lap up owre our fauld-dyke,
   And dighted his red-wat mou.

I' the very third lilt o' that sweet sang,
   Red lowed the new-woke moon ;
The stars drapped blude on the yellow gowan tap,
   Sax miles roun' that maiden.

" I hae dwalt on the Nith," quo' the young Cowehill,
   " Thae twenty years an' three;
But the sweetest sang e'er brake frae a lip,
   Comes thro' the greenwood to me.

O is it a voice frae twa earthlie lips,
   Whilk makes sic melodie ?
It wad wyle† the lark frae the morning lift,
   And weel may it wyle me ! "

---

* *Forhood*, forsook.　　　　† *Wyle*, entice.

" I dreamed a dreary thing, master,
　　Whilk I am rad ye rede ;
　I dreamed ye kissed a pair o' sweet lips,
　　That drapped o' red heart's-blude."

" Come haud my steed, ye little foot-page,
　　Shod wi' the red gowd roun' ;
　Till I kiss the lips whilk sing sae sweet,"
　　An' lightlie lap he down.

" Kiss nae the singer's lips, master,
　　Kiss nae the singer's chin ;
　Touch nae her hand," quo' the little foot-page,
　　" If skaithless hame ye'd win.

O wha will sit on yere toom saddle,
　　O wha will bruik yere gluve ;
　An' wha will fauld yere erled * bride,
　　I' the kindlie clasps o' luve ? "

He took aff his hat, a' gowd i' the rim,
　　Knot wi' a siller ban';
　He seemed a' in lowe † wi' his gowd raiment,
　　As thro' the green wood he ran.

" The simmer-dew fa's saft, fair maid,
　　Aneath the siller moon ;
　But eerie is thy seat i' the rock,
　　Washed wi' the white sea faem.

---

* *Erled*, betrothed.　　　　† *In lowe*, in a blaze.

Come wash me wi' thy lilie white hand,
   Below and 'boon the knee ;
An' I'll kame thae links o' yellow burning gowd,
   Aboon thy bonnie blue ee.

How rosie are thy parting lips,
   How lilie-white thy skin,
An' weel I wat thae kissing een
   Wad tempt a saint to sin."

" Tak aff thae bars an' bobs o' gowd,
   Wi' thy gared doublet fine ;
An' thraw me aff thy green mantle,
   Leafed wi' the siller twine.

An' a' in courtesie fair knight,
   A maiden's mind to win,
The gowd lacing o' thy green weeds,
   Wad harm her lilie skin."

Syne coost he aff his green mantle,
   Hemm'd wi' the red gowd roun' ;
His costly doublet coost he aff,
   Wi' red gowd flow'red down.

" Now ye maun kame my yellow hair,
   Down wi' my pearlie kame ;
Then rowe me in thy green mantle,
   An' tauk me maiden hame."

" But first come tauk me 'neath the chin,
   An' syne come kiss my cheek ;

An' spread my hanks o' wat'ry hair,
　　I' the new-moon beam to dreep."

Sae first he kissed her dimpled chin,
　　Syne kissed her rosie cheek ;
And lang he wooed her willin' lips,
　　Like hether-hinnie sweet !

"O ! if ye'll come to the bonnie Cowehill,
　　'Mang primrose banks to woo,
I'll wash thee ilk day i' the new milked milk,
　　An' bind wi' gowd yere brow.

An' a' for a drink o' the clear water
　　Ye'se hae the rosie wine,
An' a' for the water white lilie,
　　Ye'se hae these arms o' mine."

" But what 'll she say, yere bonnie young bride
　　Busked wi' the siller fine ;
Whan the rich kisses ye kept for her lips,
　　Are left wi' vows on mine ? "

He took his lips frae her red-rose mou',
　　His arm frae her waist sae sma';
" Sweet maiden, I'm in brydal speed,
　　It's time I were awa.

O gie me a token o' luve, sweet May,
　　A leal love token true ; "
She crapped a lock o' yellow gowden hair,
　　An' knotted it roun' his brow.

" O tie nae it sae strait, sweet May,
 But wi' luve's rose-knot kynde ;
My head is fu' o' burning pain,
 O saft ye maun it bynde."

His skin turned a' o' the red-rose hue,
 Wi' draps o' bludie sweat ;
An' he laid his head 'mang the water lilies,
 " Sweet maiden, I maun sleep."

She tyed ae link o' her wat yellow hair,
 Aboon his burning bree ;*
Amang his curling haffet locks
 She knotted knurles three.

She weaved owre his brow the white lilie,
 Wi' witch-knots mae than nine ;
" Gif ye were seven times bride-groom owre,
 This night ye shall be mine."

O twice he turned his sinking head,
 An' twice he lifted his ee ;
O twice he sought to lift the links
 Were knotted owre his bree.

" Arise, sweet knight, yere young bride waits,
 An' doubts her ale will sowre ;
An' wistly looks at the lilie white sheets,
 Down spread in ladie-bowre."

---

* *Bree*, the brow.

2 A

An' she has prenned* the broidered silk,
　　About her white hause bane ;
Her princely petticoat is on,
　　Wi' gowd can stan' its lane.

He faintlie, slowlie, turned his cheek,
　　And faintly lift his ee,
And he strave to lowse the witching bands
　　Aboon his burning bree.

Then took she up his green mantle
　　Of lowing gowd the hem ;
Then took she up his silken cap,
　　Rich wi' a siller stem ;
An' she threw them wi' her lilie hand
　　Amang the white sea faem.

She took the bride ring frae his finger
　　An' threw it in the sea ;
" That hand shall mense† nae ither ring
　　But wi' the will o' me."

She faulded him i' her lilie arms,
　　An' left her pearlie kame ;
His fleecy locks trailed owre the sand
　　As she took the white sea-faem.

First raise the star out owre the hill,
　　An' neist the lovelier moon ;
While the beauteous bride o' Gallowa'
　　Looked for her blythe bride-groom.

---

* *Prenned,* pinned.　　　† *To mense,* to grace.

Lythlie she sang while the new-moon raise,
    Blythe as a young bryde May,
Whan the new-moon lights her lamp o' luve,
    An' blinks the bryde away.

" Nithsdale, thou art a gay garden,
    Wi' monie a winsome flower ;
But the princeliest rose o' that garden
    Maun blossom in my bower.

An' I will kepp* the drapping dew
    Frae my red rose's tap,
An' the balmy blobs o' ilka leaf,
    I'll kepp them drap by drap.
An' I will wash my white bosom
    A' wi' this heavenly sap."

An' ay she sewed her silken snood,
    An' sung a brydal sang ;
But aft the tears drapt frae her ee,
    Afore the gray morn cam.

The sun lowed ruddie 'mang the dew,
    Sae thick on bank and tree ;
The plow-boy whistled at his darg,†
    The milk-may answered hie ;

---

* *To kepp*, to catch, to receive in the act of falling.   Thus Burns—
       " Mourn, Spring, thou darling of the year !
        Ilk cowslip cup shall *kep* a tear."
† *At his darg*, at his work.

But the lovelie bride o' Gallowa'
    Sat wi' a wat-shod* ee.

Ilk breath o' wind 'mang the forest leaves
    She heard the bridegroom's tongue,
And she heard the brydal-coming lilt
    In every bird which sung.

She sat high on the tap towre stane,
    Nae waiting May was there ;
She lowsed the gowd busk frae her breast,
    The kame frae 'mang her hair ;
She wiped the tear-blobs frae her ee,
    An' looked lang and sair !

First sang to her the blythe wee bird,
    Frae aff the hawthorn green ;
" Loose out the love curls frae yere hair,
    Ye plaited sae weel yestreen."

An' the spreckled woodlark frae 'mang the clouds
    O' heaven came singing down ;
" Tauk out the bride-knots frae yere hair
    An' let thae lang locks down."

" Come, byde wi' me, ye pair o' sweet birds,
    Come down an' byde wi' me ;
Ye sall peckle o' the bread an' drink o' the wine,
    An' gowd yere cage sall be."

---

* " *Wat-shod* " is a phrase peculiar to Dumfrieshire and Galloway. " *Bless the bairn, its een's wat-shod*," is the mother's cry when she finds her child's eyes brimful of tears. Among the peasantry it has an endearing and familiar sweetness—perhaps from frequent usage, and being a traditional phrase.

She laid the bride-cake 'neath her head,
   An' syne below her feet ;
An' laid her down 'tween the lilie-white sheets,
   An' soundlie did she sleep !

It was i' the mid-hour o' the night,
   Her siller-bell did ring ;
An' soun't as if nae earthlie hand
   Had pou'd the silken string.

There was a cheek touch'd that ladye's,
   Cauld as the marble stane ;
An' a hand cauld as the drifting snaw
   Was laid on her breast-bane.

" O cauld is thy hand, my dear Willie,
   O cauld, cauld is thy cheek ;
An' wring thae locks o' yellow hair,
   Frae which the cauld draps dreep."

" O seek anither bridegroom, Marie,
   On thae bosom-faulds to sleep ;
My bride is the yellow water lilie,
   Its leaves my brydal sheet !"

This romantic and affecting ballad was transmitted to the Editor by *Jean Walker*, a young girl of Galloway, who preserved the songs "She's gane to dwall in Heaven," "Thou hast sworn by thy God, my Jeanie," "The Pawkie Loon the Miller," and "Young Derwentwater." The following extract from a note accompanying it may be an illustrative specimen of the language and ideas of Scottish peasants.

"TO MR. CROMEK.

* * * * "A weed turns a flower when its set in a garden. Will these Songs be better or bonnier in print? I enclose you a flower new pou'd frae the banks of blythe Cowehill. It has long grown almost unkend of. Gentility disnae pou' a flower that blumes i' the fields;—it is trampled on for a weed when it's no in a flower-pot. I see you smiling at the witching lilts of the sweet-singing Mermaid. Well, come again to Galloway. Sit down i' the gloaming dewfall on the green merse side, amang the flowers; and if a pair of lilie arms, and twa kissing lips, and witching een, forbye the sweet movement of a honey dropping tongue, winna gaur ye believe in the lilting glamour of the Mermaid, ye may gang back to England, singing—"Praise be blest!" How will your old fashioned taste, and the new fangledness of the public's agree about these old Songs?—But tell me, can a song become old when the ideas and imagery it contains are drawn from nature? While gowans grow on our braes, and lilies on our burn-banks, so long will natural imagery and natural sentiment flourish green in song.

"I am perhaps too partial to these old Songs;—It is because they recal the memory of parental endearments: the posies of our fathers and our mothers I hold it not seemly for a daughter to let wither."

———

That the peasantry of Scotland possess a greater portion of natural taste and information than the vulgar class of any other nation is considered paradoxical by their unbelieving brethren on this side the Tweed. Were evidence required to establish this fact, a Scottish peasant would exclaim—" Where are your Ballads and Songs, the beauteous fugitives of neglected or unknown rustic bards ? Where are your sacred reliques of poetic devotion with which every Scotchman's heart is filled ?—the plaint of despair, the uplifting raptures of love, or the heart-warming lament of domestic misfortune ? With us they live ; with you they have never existed, or have perished ! "

APPENDIX.

APPENDIX.

SCOTTISH GAMES (A.) p. 8.

"ENGLAND AND SCOTLAND."

THIS boyish amusement seems to have had its origin from the more deadly games which our forefathers play-ed upon the borders. The boys cast lots till they are equally divided, and a king is chosen as leader of either party. The boundary of the kingdoms is then fixed, and marked out with small wooden pins, and a warden is placed by each party to keep those marks unmoved. A small ring is then described, at an hundred paces dis-tance from the boundary ; this is His Majesty's capital, where his treasure, represented by the boys' hats or coats, is deposited.

War being declared, every eye is on the alert ;—the parties marshal upon the borders, make feints of attack, while some of the boldest attempt to bear away His Ma-jesty's treasure. If the intruder be caught on the hostile ground he is *taend*, that is, clapped three times on the head, which makes him a prisoner. He is set down within the circle of the capital, nor dares to forfeit his pass of honour unless relieved by some of his country-men. This retaking is accomplished by touching the party with the hand, he gets free, and tries to accomplish his retreat. To relieve a prisoner, and pillage with impunity, is reckoned a notable exploit.

The game is finished when those of one kingdom carry off the other's bonnets and coats, keeping their own secure. This curious game somewhat resembles the pilfering Border warfare of old, and may be considered an excellent satire on the struggles of nations for petty rivers, and paltry dukedoms.

"THE OUTS AND THE INS."

This game is peculiar to the low countries of Scotland, and is very common in Nithsdale and Galloway.

It seems to be formed from the mutability of Border inheritance, and is the "Debateable Land" which so often caused the English bows and the Scottish broad swords to be drawn. Our forefathers seem to have directed the sports of their children to the practice of stratagem and plunder; and this remnant of other times was the miniature of deadlier games, and disciplined youth to the bloody play which awaited them in manhood. A circle is drawn and neatly divided into six parts; on one of these is cut another circle of ten feet diameter,—this is called the "Ins," and the large circle is called the "Outs." A stone, or branch of a tree, is set up at these marks in the large circle;—these are termed "Dools." The boys divide in equal numbers and cast lots for the Ins, which is the seat of glory and heroism. The fortunate party all step into the Ins, and the other party run to the Outs ; a boy then steps forth from either side. To begin the game,—the boy in the Outs throws a ball of yarn covered with leather or party-coloured thread so as gently to light on the other's hand, who stands with it open, and his arm in a swinging attitude, in order to strike the ball. This he does with great dexterity, avoiding the outer party, and preventing them from catching it as it flies : which, should one of them catch, loses the Ins. The boy, on striking away the ball, runs to the first dool, and touches it with his foot. One of his fellows stands forth in the Ins, striking back the ball, while his partner gains another dool, and so on till he recovers the Ins. The other one who struck away the ball in his absence runs the same career. But should the ball be caught, or while he is running to reach his dool, should he be struck by the ball from the outer party, the Ins are lost, and the enemy rushes in to the evacuated dominions, and again the game goes on.

A more youthful game than this, but evidently of the same origin, is common, I believe, on the borders of either kingdom, called " Keep the Castle," by the Eng-lish, and " Haud the Bowerique," by the Scotch. One boy takes possession of a little knowe top, or hillock, from which his fellows attempt to dislodge him. Whenever he is pushed off his conquerer succeeds, and this is repeated until one of them reigns king beyond the power of dethroning.

APPENDIX (B.) p. 17.

The following affecting narrative is taking fron the life of Peden, and though it has had a very extensive circulation, from the circumstance of its being quoted in the notes to Mr. Grahame's popular poem of " The Sabbath," yet it exemplifies so strongly the severe persecutions which the Presbyterians endured, that no apology need be given for its insertion in this place.

"One morning, between five and six hours, John Brown, having performed the worship of God in his family, was going with a spade in his hand to make ready some peat-ground. The mist being very dark, he knew not till the bloody Claverhouse compassed him with three troops of horse, brought him to his house, and there examined him ; who, though he was a man of stammering speech, yet answered him distinctly and solidly ; which made Claverhouse to examine those whom he had taken to be his guides through the muirs, if they had heard him preach ? They answered, " No, no, he was never a preacher." He said, " If he has never preached, meikle has he prayed in his time." He said to John, " Go to your prayers, for you shall immediately die." When he was praying Claverhouse interrupted him three times : one time that he stopped him he was praying that the Lord would spare a remnant, and not make a full end in the day of his anger. Claverhouse said, " I gave you time to pray, and you are begun to preach ;" he turned about on his knees, and said, " Sir, you know neither the nature of praying nor preaching that calls this preaching ;" then continued, without confusion. When ended, Claverhouse said, " Take good night of your wife and children." His wife standing by with her children in her arms that she had brought forth to him, and another child of his first wife's, he came to her and said, " Now, Marion, the day is come, that I told you would come, when I first spake to you of marrying me." She said, " Indeed, John, I can willingly part with you." Then he said, " This is all I desire ; I have no more to do but to die.'' He kissed his wife and bairns, and wished purchased and promised blessings to be multiplied on them, and his blessing. Claverhouse ordered six soldiers to shoot him ; the most part of the bullets came upon his head, which scattered his brains upon the ground. Claverhouse said to his wife, " What thinkest thou of thy husband now, woman ?" She said, "I thought ever much of him, and now as much as ever." He said, "it were justice to lay thee beside him." She said, " If ye were permitted, I doubt not but your cruelty would go that length ; but how will ye make answer for this morning's work." He said, "To man I can be answerable; and for God, I will take him in mine own hand." Claverhouse mounted on his horse, and left her with the corpse of her dead husband lying there; she set the bairn on the ground, and gathered his brains, and tied up his head, and straighted his body, and covered him with her plaid, and sat down, and wept over him. It being a very desert place, where never victual grew, and far from neighbours, it was some time before any friends came to her : the first that came was a very fit hand, that old singular Christian woman, in the Cummerhead, named Elizabeth Menzies, three miles distant, who had been tried with the violent death of her husband at Pentland, afterwards of two worthy sons, Thomas Weir, who was killed at Drumclog, and David Steel, who was suddenly shot afterwards when taken. The said Marion Weir, sitting upon her husband's grave, told me, that, before that, she could see no blood but she was in danger to faint, and yet she was helped to be a witness to all this, without either fainting or confusion; except when the shots were let off, her eyes were dazzled. His corpse was buried at the end of his house, where he was slain.— PEDEN'S LIFE, *p. 21.*

APPENDIX (C.) p. 18.

"TAKING THE BEUK."

To describe this sublime ceremony of devotion to God, a picture of the Cottar's Ha', taken from the more primitive times of rustic simplicity, will be most expressive and effectual.

On entering a neat thatched cottage, when past the partition or hallan, a wide, far projecting chimney piece, garnished with smoked meat, met your eye. The fire, a good space removed from the end wall, was placed against a large whinstone, called the cat-hud. Behind this was a bench stretching along the gable, which, on trysting nights, was occupied by the children; the best seat being courteously proffered to strangers. The Cottar Sire was placed on the left of the fire, removed from the bustle of housewifery.—A settee of oak, antiquely carved and strewn with favourite texts of scripture, was the good man's seat, where he rested after the day's fatigue, nursing and instructing his children. His library shelf above him displayed his folio Bible, covered with rough calf skin, wherein were registered his children's names and hour of birth; some histories of the old reforming worthies, (divines who waded through the blood and peril of persecution), the sacred books of his fathers lay carefully adjusted and pretty much used : and the acts and deeds of Scotland's saviour, Wallace,

2 C

and the immortal Bruce, were deemed worthy of holding a place among the heroic divines who had won the heavenly crown of martyrdom.   Above these were hung a broad sword and targe, the remains of ancient warfare, which happily the hand of peace had long forgot to wield.——From the same pin depended the kirn-cut of corn,* curiously braided and adorned with ribbons. Beside him was his fowling-piece, which, before the enaction of Game Laws, supplied his family with venison and fowls in their season.   At the end of the langsettle was the window, which displayed a few panes of glass and two oaken boards, that opened like shutters, for the admission of air.   On the gudewife's side appeared her articles of economy and thrift.   A dresser, replenished with pewter plates, with a large meal chest of carved oak, extended along the side wall; bunches of yarn hung from a loft or flooring, made of small wood or ryse, spread across the joisting, and covered with moor turf.   The walls, white with lime, were garnished with dairy utensils (every Cottar almost having one or two kye).   At each side of the middle entry was a bed, sometimes of very curious and ingenious workmanship, being posted with oak, and lined with barley straw, finely cleaned and inwoven with thread; these were remarkably warm and much valued.

---

* The name sometimes given to the last handful of grain cut down on the harvest field.

Family worship was performed every evening, but on the Sabbath morning it was attended with peculiar solemnity. At that season all the family, and frequently some of the neighbours, presented themselves before the aged village apostle. He seated himself on the lang-settle, laying aside his bonnet and plaid. His eldest child came submissively forward, and unclasping the Bible, placed it across his father's knees. After a few minutes of religious silence, he meekly lifts his eyes over his family to mark if they are all around him, and decorous. Opening the Bible he says— in a tone of simple and holy meekness—" Let us reverently worship our God by singing the (eighth) Psalm." He reads it aloud ; then gives or recites line after line, leading the tune himself. The *Martyrs* is a chosen air, so called in honour of those men who displayed a zeal worthy of the name, and perished in the persecution. All the family join in this exquisitely mournful tune till the sacred song is finished. A selected portion of scripture is then read from the sub-lime soarings of Isaiah, or the solemn morality of Job. As the divine precepts of his Saviour are the sacred rules by which the good man shapes the conduct of his chil-dren, Isaiah's fifty-third chapter, where the coming of the Redeemer is foretold, is the soul-lifting favourite of rustic devotion. It is read with an exalted inspiration of voice, accordant with the subject. The family rise as he clasps the book, fall down on their knees, bowing their heads to the ground.   The good man, kneeling over his Bible, pours his prayer to heaven in a strain of feeling and fervent eloquence.   His severity of church discipline relaxes in the warmth of his heart,—" May our swords become plowshares, and our spears reaping hooks :— May all find grace before thee !"

There is not perhaps a more impressive scene than a Scottish Sabbath morn presents, when the wind is low, the summer sun newly risen, and all the flocks at browse by the waters and by the woods :—how glorious then to listen to the holy murmur of retired prayer, and the dis- tant chaunt of the Cottarman's psalm spreading from hamlet and village !

This noble scene has been painted in never-fading colours by the vigorous and masterly genius of Burns. It was a subject dear to his heart ;—a parental scene. He has touched it with the poetic inspiration of divine rapture, and with the fidelity of truth itself.

" The cheerfu' supper done, wi' serious face,
    They, round the ingle, form a circle wide ;
The sire turns o'er, wi' patriarchal grace,
    The big *ha'-Bible*, ance his father's pride :
His bonnet rev'rently is laid aside,
    His lyart haffets wearing thin an' bare ;
Those strains that once did sweet in Zion glide,
    He wales a portion with judicious care ;
And ' Let us worship God !' he says, with solemn air."

APPENDIX (D.) p. 25.

A DESCRIPTION OF THE STOOL OF REPENTANCE.

Though this vile stool of repentance is sufficiently familiar to the good people of Scotland, yet some explanation of its uses may be required by the English reader; and, as the Editor considers himself pledged to give every illustration he has been able to collect of Scottish manners and customs, the following account will not be deemed misplaced.

When the disastrous and bloody struggle of Scottish reformation was over, and the wretched hovels of covenanting Calvinism rose among the majestic ruins of Romish devotion, all that escaped the wreck of original genius and peculiar cast of character, was the "Stool of Repentance.* It was an engine of terror well suited to Knox's stern and rigorous discipline, as it gave him a severe control over the looseness of the times, and enabled him to apply the merciless rod of church-censure against the

---

* There is a remark in Burns' unpublished MS. Journal of his excursion from Edinburgh to the Highlands, not inapplicable to this subject. It is amusing to observe how bitterly he vents his antipathies whenever an instance of superstitious tyranoy occurs, repugnant to liberal feelings; and it must bave been highly diverting to witness his soliloquy on the present occasion.

"Linlithgow ———————— A pretty good old gothic church—the *infamous Stool of Repentance* standing in the old Romish way, on a lofty situation.

"What a poor, pimping business is a Presbyterian place of worship! dirty, narrow, and squalid; stuck in a corner of old Popish grandeur such as Linlithgow, and much more Melrose!—Ceremony and show, if judiciously thrown in, are absolutely necessary for the bulk of mankind, both in religious and civil matters."

vices even of the nobility.   Such, probably, was his
motive for raking this vile stool from the ruins of the
fallen church.   It has ever been extremely obnoxious to
the free spirit of the peasantry ; in proof of which many
of their songs might be adduced, if their delicacy were
equal to their wit and humour.——The reply of an old
woman to Mr. Knox, is worthy of record.   After holding
forth in praise of the *goodlie wark o' reformation*, as he
termed it, and railing against the wickedness of popery,
he zealously exclaimed, " I hae plucked the raiment frae
the harlot!"   "Ah, na, na!" quo' the good dame, point-
ing to the chair of repentance, "ye hae keepit the vera
tassel o' the breeks o' Popery."   This stool of terror was
fashioned like an arm-chair, and was raised on a pedestal,
nearly two feet higher than the other seats, directly front-
ing the pulpit.   When the kirk-bell was rung, the culprit
ascended the chair, and the bellman arrayed him in the
black sackcloth gown of fornication.   Here he stood
three Sundays successively, his face uncovered, and the
awful scourge of unpardoning divinity hung over him.
The women stood here in the same accoutrements, and
were denied the privilege of a veil :

> " A fixed figure for the hand of scorn,
>   To point his slow unmoving finger at."

The punishment of this humiliating exaltation was not
inflicted on illegitimate parents only, but also on those

who healed the breach of chastity by subsequent marriage. So scrupulous was covenanting kirk in this respect, that the bridegroom had to lodge *six pounds Scots*, in the custody of the Session, as a pledge against unwedded incontinence, which, if convicted, he forfeited. This tax was broadly termed by the peasantry, in allusion to the border taxes, " Buttock mail." The severity of these punishments, so repugnant to female delicacy, and to the sweet, innocent modesty of the girls of Scotland, has however of late years been relaxed ; in many places they are commuted for small fines, and private admonition. It is enough for incontinence to walk over the burning plow-shares of its own repentant feelings, without being cast bound into the seven-times heated furnace of Calvinism. Highly to the honour of the Scottish clergy and people, these stepping stools to child-murder are now almost universally swept out of the churches. Such an epithet may be deemed a harsh one, but the following truly affecting song fully justifies it, and seems purposely written to touch the heart of religious tenderness with the simple and pathetic eloquence of unwedded and abandoned sorrow.

" There* sat ' mang the flowers a fair ladie,
Sing ohon, ohon and ohon O !

---

*There are many variations of this affecting tale. One of them appears in the *Musical Museum*, and is there called " *Fine Flowers of the Valley*," of which the present is either the original or a parallel song : I am inclined to think it is the original.

And there she has born a sweet babie
  Adown by the greenwode side O !
An' strait she rowed its swaddling band,
  Sing ohon, ohon and ohon O !
An' O ! nae mother grips took her hand
  Adown by the greenwode side O !

O twice it lifted its bonnie wee ee,
  Sing ohon, &c.
" Thae looks gae through the saul o' me,
  Adown, &c.
She buried the bonnie babe 'neath the brier,
  Sing ohon, &c.
And washed her hands wi' mony a tear,
  Adown, &c.

And as she kneelt to her God in prayer,
  Sing ohon, &c.
The sweet wee babe was smiling there,
  Adown, &c.
O ay, my God, as I look to thee,
  Sing ohon, &c.
My babe's atween my God and me,
  Adown, &c.

Ay, ay, it lifts its bonnie wee ee,
  Sing ohon, &c.
" Sic kindness get as ye shawed me,"
  Adown, &c.
An' O its smiles wad win me in,
  Sing ohon, &c.
But I'm borne down by deadly sin,
  Adown, &c."

Never was there a punishment devised which so completely defeated its own purpose.   It either hardened
or broke the heart of the sufferer.   Without allowance
for the different degrees of guilt in different cases, or for
the relative situation of the parties in the same case, it
was inflicted with indiscriminate and unmitigated rigour

on the male and the female transgressor,—on the seducer
and the seduced. He, driven by exposure to blunt the
poignancy of his shame in assumed effrontery, soon
banished the wholesome feelings of remorse, and by an
effort of fortitude, converted his disgrace into a triumph;
while the soft, gentle-hearted female, on whom the consequences of the trespass are, by nature and by the usages
of society, made to constitute a penance of the most
fearful and soul-subduing kind; she, in whose mind the
gloom of desertion was deepened by the loss of fame,
the alienation of those she held most dear, and the close
of every bright prospect in life; she, already the dupe
and the victim of treachery and falsehood, was held forth
as the object of unsympathising cruelty and derision. If
there be a state of mind in which

" present fears
Are less than horrible imaginings,

it is surely in the anticipation of this hateful exposure;
nor are we to wonder that an unfortunate, goaded to
despair by the dread of so barbarous, so harrowing a
punishment, should, in the fever of apprehension, stifle the
feelings of a mother, and brave the guilt of infanticide,
rather than submit to the torture of being publicly and
indelibly branded with infamy. The train of heart-
breaking circumstances which follow the disgrace; the
distant civility and coldly averted look of friends; the
dumb despairing affliction of parents; the vile fingers

D 2

of public mockery wagged at them in the streets;—are
not these excruciating punishments due only to the confirmed in vice, to the sworn votaries of prostitution ? and
must the pastors of the Church, when they should pri-
vately administer the balm of forgiveness ; when they
should go into the wilderness and seek for the lamb that
had gone astray—must they unfeelingly forbid her return
to the flock and shut the door of the fold against her for
ever ! Such Pharisaical rigour is contrary to the benevolent spirit of Christianity : far from striving to reclaim
those who are lost, it freezes all the charities of the heart,
and substitutes hypocrisy for sincere repentance. But
never are the iron features of puritanical stoicism more
hideous than when they frown vengeance on the lovely
face of blushing modesty, rendered more timorous by
the consciousness of a trespass ; never is the breath of
Calvinistic denunciation more repulsive than when it
blasts the flower already blighted, and drooping for want
of shelter and support. In defiance of the dictates of
common sense, and in outrage of the feelings of humanity,
this engine of monkish despotism was preserved by the
Reformers, and became more terrible in their hands than
in those of its inventors, until the liberal spirit of the
present age prevailed over the narrow bigotry of fanaticism,
and consigned the *cutty-stool* to the oblivion it had long
merited. Ridicule contributed, perhaps more powerfully
than reason, to bring it into disuse. The rough, manly

wit of *Butler*, and the bold energetic humour of *Burns* have done more to correct the pedantry of religion than whole volumes of serious expostulation.

APPENDIX (E) p. 53.

HISTORY OF WITCHCRAFT, SKETCHED FROM THE POPULAR TALES OF THE PEASANTRY OF NITHSDALE AND GALLOWAY.

" These emissaries of Satan, with the stamp of hell's chosen on their foreheads," as a reforming saint once called them, have long held uncontrolled dominion in Galloway and in the Pot of Nith, as the peasantry term that beautiful vale in which the Burgh of Dumfries stands.

Though religion has triumphed over their most daring spells, yet there are remains of their influence still in unsubdued force, over which scriptural light and reforming reason have not prevailed. The strong sense and adherence to religious duty—their belief in and familiar acquaintance with scripture (the inheritance of the Scottish peasantry) will preserve and transmit this remnant of heathenism to the latest posterity. Speak doubtingly of witchcraft to a peasant, he produces his Bible, and who dare doubt the evidence of heaven ! The knowledge which the Reformation poured on the mind swept away many superstitions, but witchcraft remained untouched. To counteract the looser and corrupt manners of the Catholic clergy, the new religion assumed a persecuting strictness of discipline, and enforced her iron laws to drive familiar spirits and wizards from the land. Old men and women were hurried to the stake, and to the scaffold, and martyred on their own confession. Trifling evidence, in cases of unconfessing stubbornness, was proof sufficient. A wish of ill luck, expressed in anger, and partly fulfilled, perhaps for a bloody purpose, convicted the poor offender of dealings with the *foul fiend,* and almost convinced the guiltless mind of the wretched sufferers that hell had been busy in their hearts, and had possessed them with diabolical craft, which they had unwittingly used. Insensible marks, which the second-sighted searchers of witchcraft called "little uncommon figures of strawberry leaves," &c., &c., found on the human frame, were construed into the seal of Satan, and taken for notable proofs of familiar agency. So eager were they to destroy Satan's dominion on earth, that the bloodhounds of religious law were uncoupled, and witches were hunted down by their very smell. Wild exaggerated tales of devilish artifice were collected and published by visionary enthusiasts, the public mind was poisoned and inflamed, and all the land was in a state of infatuation. That royal pedant, James ' the First, wielded his kingly wisdom against the power of the devil, and enriched his country with his most notable book on witchcraft. During the reign of his unfortunate son, and in the turbulent time of the commonwealth, the public mind adventured in a bloodier field, and the Church had to unsheath her sword in a more mortal contest.

The restored unfeeling and licentious Charles filled the land with persecutions and massacre; witchcraft was then little heeded, overpowered by greater calamity: —the free charter of Conscience, after a fierce struggle, was gained by the Revolution, and we hear little more of punishment awaiting on witchcraft.

The following broken outline of Scottish witchcraft is selected from the faithful records of tradition, which is the surest book for the unfolding of character and general opinion.

Witchcraft being no inheritance of blood, but the immediate gift of the devil, has been, by his artifice, always bestowed on those who could make most judicious use of it, for the annoyance of the righteous, and the futherance of perdition. With uniform consistency, he has enriched by his knowledge, and exalted by his power, the *low scum* of creation only—the *peasantry*. Well he knew that craft, ambition, and pride, belonged to *hereditary greatness*, which, from his own example, would have waxed mighty in his knowledge and disputed his empire,

making (to use the rough phrase) " Hell too hot for him."
Thus he loved to dwell among the old, the weak, and the
illiterate ; though he seems occasionally to have taken
much delight and high edification in conversing with his
younger proselytes.

From the gigantic ruins of his empire (which still remain in the breath of tradition) the poet of Scotland has
been led to lift up his voice, and cry,

> " Far ken'd and noted is thy name !"

With the foresight of a lawgiver, Satan established and
promulgated laws, made ordinances, and set apart certain times for infernal delight and revelry.

Trystes, where the whole Warlocks and Witches of a
country were assembled, are yet remembered among the
peasantry with terror ; they were wont to date their age
from them ; thus—" I was christened o' the Sunday
after *Tibbie Fleucher's* Hallowmass rade."

The noted tryste of the Nithsdale and Galloway Warlocks and Witches was held on a rising knowe, four miles
distant from Dumfries, called " *Locher-brigg Hill*." There
are yet some fragments of the Witches' *Gathering Hymn*,
too characteristically curious to be omitted.

> " When the gray Howlet has three times hoo'd,
> When the grimy Cat has three times mewed,
> When the Tod has yowled three times i' the wode,
> At the red moon cowering ahin the clud ;

When the stars hae cruppen' deep i' the drift,
Lest Cantrips had pyked them out o' the lift,
Up horsies a', but mair adowe,
Ryde, ryde, for *Locher-brigg knowe!*

Roused by this infernal summons, the earth and the air groaned with the unusual load. It was a grand though a daring attempt for man, or aught of mortal frame, to view this diabolical hurry. The wisest part barred their doors, and left the world to its own misrule. Those aged matrons, deep read in incantation, says tradition, "could sit i' the coat tails o' the moon," or harness the wind to their rag-weed chariot;—could say to the west star, "byde thou me!" or to the moon, "hynte me in thy arm, for I am weary!" Those Carlins of garrulous old age, who had suffered martyrdom on the brow for the cause, rode on chosen broom-sticks, shod with murdered men's bones. These moved spontaneously to the will of the possessor; but the more gay and genteel kimmers loved a softer seat than the bark of a broomstick. A bridle shreded from the skin of an unbaptized infant, with bits forged in Satan's armoury, possessed irresistible power when shaken above any living thing. Two young lads of Nithsdale once served a widow dame, who possessed a bridle with these dangerous qualifications. One of them, a plump, merry young fellow, suddenly lost all his gaiety, and became lean, as if "*ridden post by a witch.*" On his neighbour lad's inquiry about the cause, he only said, "Lie at the bed stock an' ye'll be as lean as me."

It was on a Hallowmass ee'n, and though he felt unusual drowsiness, he kept himself awake. At midnight, his mistress cautiously approaching his bed-side, shook the charmed bridle over his face, saying, "*Up Horsie*," when to his utter astonishment, he arose in the form of a gray horse! The cantrip bit was put in his teeth, and, mounted by the Carlin, he went off like the wind. Feeling the prick of infernal spur, he took such leaps and bounds, that he reached Locherbrigg knowe in a few moments. He was fastened by the bridle to a tree, with many more of his acquaintance, whom he recognized through their brutal disguise. He looked petrified with affright when the Father of Cantrips drew a circle around the *knowe*, within which no baptized brow could enter. All being assembled, hands were joined, and a ring of Warlocks and Witches danced in the enchanted bound with many lewd and uncouth gestures. In the centre he beheld a thick smoke, and presently arose the piercing yells and screams of hellish baptism, which the new converts were enduring. Startled and terrified to furious exertion, he plunged, pulled, and reared; and praying ardently to Heaven, he shook off the bridle of power,— and starting up in his own shape he seized the instrument of his transformation. It was now gray day light when the conclave dispersed, for their orgies could not endure the rebuke of the sun. He watched his mistress, who, all haste and confusion, was hurrying to her steed; shaking the bridle over her brow, she started up a "gude gray mare," and was hastened home with such push of spur that all competitors were left far behind! The sun was nigh risen as he hurried into the stable. Pulling off the bridle, his cantrip-casting mistress appeared with hands and feet lacerated with travel, and her sides pricked to the bone. On her rider's promising never to divulge his night adventure, she allowed him to keep the bridle as a pledge of safety.

To ride post on the human body was a privilege enjoyed only by those who paramoured with Satan, or had done some signal feat. Many of these grovelling hags, to escape the detection of their neighbours, had to belie the form of God in the unholy semblance of cats. The import of these meetings is now indistinctly known, and popular report wanders in uncertainty. It is hinted, from glimpses gotten by daring wights, that "*Kain Bairns*" were paid to Satan, and fealty done for reigning through his division of Nithsdale and Galloway. These *Kain Bairns* were the fruit of their wombs; though sometimes the old barren hags stole the unchristened offspring of their neighbours to fill the hellish treasury. Their rite of baptism was still ranker of glamour; so much so, that the voice of tradition "speaks lowne" when describing it. They were stripped naked, and the hellish hieroglyphic was impressed on their sides and bosoms. It has puzzled the wise to decypher these characters, else deeper insight into the laws and civil government of our arch enemy might perhaps have been acquired; but this unknown language was proof enough to roast the possesssor.

While this Satanic hieroglyphic was writing upon them, their yells were horrible; but the healing ointment of perdition was poured on it and allayed the smart. These marks secured them from outward ailment, and from being assailed by the dint of mortal arms. Jackets, woven of water snake skins, at a certain time of a March moon, were much in vogue among the crusading servants of Satan; and are yet remembered by the name of *warlock feckets*. Tradition has arrayed the brave persecutor Claverhouse in a lead proof jacket. He rode through the hail of bullets unhurt, pushing on his career of victory; but at length was marked out by one of those very men whom he had proscribed and persecuted. His charmed *fecket* could not resist a "*silver sixpence*" from the mouth of a Cameronian's fusee !

Apart from these general meetings, or "Hallowmass Rades," as they are yet called, there were trysts of friendly converse and of consultation, held between a few of the presiding Carlins, where the private emolument of the parties, or the revenge of injury offered them, was amply discussed. Here drugs and charms were compounded and formed; * figures were shaped in clay of

---

* The worthy author of "*Satan's Invisible World Discovered,*" ingeniously shuffles the lewdness of Scottish Song on the devil's shoulders.

those who had encroached on their empire, which, when pierced with pins, conveyed by sympathetic feeling their maims and wounds to the person they represented.   The baking of the "Witch Cake," with its pernicious virtues, is a curious process, recorded in a traditional song, which we here give entire, to convince the fair reader that her lot is cast in safer times, when nature is the only tempter, and love the only Witch Cake.

"THE WITCH CAKE.

" I saw yestreen, I saw yestreen,
　　Little wis ye what I saw yestreen,
　　The black cat pyked out the gray ane's een,
　　At the hip o' the hemlock knowe yestreen.

Wi' her tail i' her teeth she whomel'd roun',
　　Wi' her tail i' her teeth she whomel'd roun',
　　'Till a braw star drapt frae the lift * aboon,
　　An' she keppit it e'er it wan to the grun'. †

She hynt them a' in her mow' an' chowed,
　　She hynt them a' in her mow' an' chowed,
　　She drabbled them owre wi' a black tade's blude,
　　An' baked a bannock,—an' ca'd it gude !—

She haurned it weel wi' ae blink o' the moon,
　　She haurned it weel wi' ae blink o' the moon,
　　An withre-shines thrice she whorled it roun',
　　'There's some sall skirl ere ye be done.'

"As the devil is the author of charms and spells, so is he the author of several baudy songs which are sung. A reverend minister told me, that one who was the devil's piper, a wizard, confessed to him, that at a ball of dancing, the foul spirit taught him a baudy song, to sing and play, as it were this night, and, ere two days passed, all the lads and lasses of the town were lilting it through the street. It were an abomination to rehearse it." Page 142.

* *Lift*—the sky.　　　　　　† *i.e.,* She caught it ere it fell to the ground.

' Some lass maun gae wi' a kilted sark,
Some priest maun preach in a thackless kirk ;
Thread maun be spun for a dead man's sark,
A' maun be done e'er the sang o' the lark.'

Tell nae what ye saw yestreen,
Tell nae what ye saw yestreen,
There's ane may gaur thee sich an' graen,
For telling what ye saw yestreen ! "

Caerlaverock and New Abbey are still celebrated as the native parishes of two midnight caterers in the festivals of Glamour. They were rivals in fame, in power, and dread. On the night of every full moon they met to devise employment for the coming month. Their confederacy, and their trysting haunts, had been discovered, and were revealed by chosen and holy men who ministered to their Creator and fulfilled his dictates.

Debarred from holding secret conference on the solid sward, they fixed their trysts on the unstable waters which separate their parishes. This tale, so full of character, was taken down by the Editor from the word-of-mouth evidence of the man who saw all that passed ; and it must be told in his own simple, expressive language.

" I gaed out ae fine simmer night to haud my halve at the Pow fit. It was twal' o clock, an' a' was lowne ; the moon had just gotten up——ye mought' a gathered preens ! I heard something firsle like silk——I glowered roun, an' 'lake ! what saw I but a bonnie boat, wi' a nob o' gowd, an' sails like new-coined siller. It was only but a wee bittie frae me, I mought amaist touch't it. 'Gude speed ye, gif ye gan for guid,' quo I, for I dreed our auld Carlin was casting some o' her pranks. Another cunning boat cam' aff frae Caerla'rick to meet it. Thae twa bade a stricken hour thegither sidie for sidie— 'Haith,' quo' I, 'the deil's grit wi' some!' sae I crap down amang some lang cowes till Luckie cam' back. The boat played bowte again the bank, an out lowpes Kimmer, wi' a pyked naigs head i' her han'. 'Lord be about us!' quo' I, for she cam' straught for me. She howked up a green turf, covered her bane, an' gaed her wa's. When I thought her hame, up I gat and pou'd up the bane and haed it. I was fley'd to gae back for twa or three nights, lest the diel's minnie should wyte me for her uncannie boat, and lair me 'mang the sludge, or may be do waur. I gaed back howsever; an' on that night o' the moon wha comes to me but Kimmer! 'Rabbin,' quo' she, 'fand ye ane auld bane amang the cowes?'—'Deed no, it may be gowd for me!' quo' I— 'Weel, weel, quo' she, I'll byde and help ye hame wi' your fish.—God's be me help, nought grippit I but tades an' paddocks! Satan, thy nieve's here, quo' I—'Ken ye (quo I) o' yon' new cheese our wyfe took but frae the chessel yestreen? I'm gaun to send't t'ye i' the morning, yere a gude neebor to me;—an' hear'st thou me! there's a bit auld bane whomeled aneath thae cowes; I kent nae it was thine. Kimmer drew't out; 'Aye,

aye, its my auld bane; weel speed ye! I' the very first
pow I gat sic a louthe o' fish that I carried 'till me back
cracked again."

These full moon meetings never boded good to the
sister parishes :—whole fields of corn would be thrashen
by the winds, and loans of kye would lowe to death;
stack yards were wholly unroofed, and sometimes there
were most alarming visitations of unwedded throes
among the poor kind hearted lasses; till the very
" Canny Wyfe" cried,—" *Enough !* "

It is a popular idea that a witch must infuse part of
her own spirit into the person or beast which she has
obtained commission to destroy. A farmer of Galloway,
coming to a new farm, with a beautiful and healthy
stock, saw them die away one by one, at stall and at
stake. His last one was lying sprawling almost in death,
when a fellow farmer got him to consider his stock as
bewitched, and attempt its relief accordingly. He placed
a pile of dried wood around his cow, setting it on fire;
the flame began to catch hold of the victim, and its outer
parts to consume, when a man, reputed to be a warlock,
came flying over the fields, yelling horribly and loudly,
conjuring the farmer to slake the fire. " Kep skaith wha
brings't," exclaimed the farmer, heaping on more fuel.
He tore his clothes in distraction, for his body was beginning to fry with the burning of his spirit. The farmer,
unwilling to drive even the devil to despair, made him

swear peace to all that was or should be his, and then unloosed his imprisoned spirit by quenching the fire.

Some farms have a powerful curse upon them, that the first of whatever stock enters the farm its kind will not prosper. To avert this some creature of a class that can best be spared is set in as a victim of atonement for its betters.

"*Ill, or uncannie een,*" rank high in the scale of witchery and glamour. These, with some, seem to be an endowment of nature ; and with others a gift from a place whence no good gifts come. Sometimes the innocent possessor of such mischievous talents would curse the very light which guided his footsteps. An old man, still remembered in Nithsdale, had *een* of such *unsonsie* glance, that they blasted the first-born of his yearly flocks, and spoiled his dairy. He would carefully shun his maids coming home with the milk at bughting time. Calves were kept from his sight, and butter was never churned in his presence ; nay his good heart kept him from ever looking man full in the face. He lived and died esteemed a pious worthy man, who possessed powers which he wished not to use ; and who never intentionally unclosed his *een* to the detriment of any living thing.

But some old women make a more judicious use of these precious endowments. When they find how much their "*uncannie* een" are respected, they sedulously seek out objects on which to exert their influence. The

wise and discerning people, instead of flying in the face
of the "*Unsonsie Carlin*," pay her tribute in secret, to
avert her glamour.   A *goan* of new milk was a bribe for
the byre ; new meal when the corn was ground, and a
dish full of groats compounded for the crops.   Did she
but once hint that her pot "*played nae brown*," a chosen
lamb or a piece of meat was presented to her in token of
friendship.   She seldom paid rent for her house, and
every young lad in the parish was anxious to cast her
peats ; so that Kimmer, according to the old Song,
"lived cantie and hale."

Before markets were so fully attended, the Lowland
wives would go at the sheep-shearing times into the Uplands, taking pieces of cloth, sugar and tea, &c. &c. for
barter in the wool traffic.   "The pawkie auld dame"
trusted to her far known character, going always empty
handed, yet she returned with the heaviest and fairest
fleeces.

The most approved charm against cantrips and spells
was a branch of rowan tree* plaited, and placed over
the byre door.   This sacred tree cannot be removed by

---

* The Mountain Ash.   Perhaps the expression in Shakspeare, " *aroynt thee,*
Witch," which has puzzled so many of his commentators, and which they have
hunted after from language to language, may have been originally written, "*a
rowan tree*, Witch "—that is, " 1 have got a rowan tree, Witch, and I fear thee
not."   It is well known that the popular superstitions of both parts of the island
were originally the same.   It requires something more than a mere knowledge
of old French or Anglo-Saxon to be a proper commentator on Shakespeare, and
many of the Scotch peasants understand some of his most difficult expressions
much better than the most learned of them.

unholy fingers.   Elfcups† were placed over stable-doors for the like purpose.   Even the mid-leg kilted daughters of Caledonia made use of charms to ward the sad effects of the witch cakes, and the kittle casts and grips to which they were often exposed.   A string of rowan-berry beads was knotted around their necks and arms ; but the witches' prophecy was necessary to be fulfilled :—

> " Some lass maun gae wi' a kilted sark ; "

for the cunning Carlin would cast knots on the lasses' coats, which took the whole skill of the " *Cannie Wife*" to unloose ! Some favoured witches were empowered with charms and spells quite removed from the common track of glamour : this is noticed in " *The Pawkie Auld Kimmer.*"

> " Kimmer can milk a hale loan o' kye,
> Yet sit at the ingle fu' snug an' fu' dry."

She possessed a sympathetic milking peg which could extract milk from any cow in the parish.

The way of restoring milk to the udders of a cow be-witched is curious, and may benefit posterity.   A young virgin milked whatever milk the cow had left, which was of bloody mixture and poisonous quality.   This was poured warm from the cow, into a brass pan, and (every inlet to the house being closed) was placed over a gentle

---

† These are little stones, perforated by friction, at a waterfall, and believed to be the workmanship of the Elves.

fire until it began to heat. Pins were dropped in, and closely stirred with a wand of rowan tree. When boiling, rusty nails were thrown in, and more fuel added. The witch instantly felt, by sympathetic power, the boiling medicine rankling through her bosom, and an awful knocking announced her arrival at the window. The sly "Guidwyfe" instantly compounded with the mother of Cantrips for "*her hale loan of kye;*" the pan was cooled, and the cows' udders swelled with genuine milk.

We will close our history of witchcraft with the only notice we could collect, of a celebrated personage, called the *Gyre Carline*; who is reckoned the mother of glamour, and near a-kin to Satan himself. She is believed to preside over the "*Hallowmass Rades;*" and mothers frequently frighten their children by threatening to give them to *M'Neven*, or the *Gyre Carline*. She is described as wearing a long gray mantle, and carrying a wand, which, like the miraculous rod of Moses, could convert water into rocks, and sea into solid land.

Lochermoss, which extends from Solway sea to Locherbrigg-hill, was once, according to tradition, an arm of the sea, and a goodly anchorage for shipping. A proud swell of the Hallowmass tide, which swept away many steeds from the Carline's assembly, so provoked her, that, baring her withered hand, she stretched over the sea her rod of power, and turned its high waves into a quagmire !

There are still carved beaks, boats, keels, and other remains of shipping, dug up in the moss at peat casting time.

APPENDIX (F) p. 98.

CHARACTER OF THE SCOTTISH LOWLAND FAIRIES, FROM THE POPULAR BELIEF OF NITHSDALE AND GALLOWAY.

The origin of Faery is involved in obscurity, but it may be traced, with great probability, to the Persians and Arabs, a people of lively and creative fancy, whose tales of the marvellous have been handed down to us in the amusing translations or the Sieµr Galland. The Persian word *Peri* bears a close affinity to the modern denomination, and the Arabian terms *Ginn* and *Ginnistan*, corresponding to our terms Fairy and Fairyland, give stronger credit to the conjecture. We may suppose the superstition to have gradually spread among the barbarians of the North of Asia and Europe, and to have mingled itself with the mythology of the Goths, from whom it has descended by tradition to their posterity, and till of late formed a part of the popular belief in every country of the western world. Marmontel, in his tale of the Sylph, takes occasion to regret its decay; and every lover of poetry

must participate in his feelings, when he remembers the
delightful reveries of Spencer, the sportive revelry of
Shakspeare, and the exquisite romance of Wieland. But
though these fantastic agents of mischief, and good-luck,
have been banished from the court and the palace, yet they
still linger in those remote abodes of simplicity and
primitive ignorance, where the torch of science has not
yet reached, or sheds doubtful and uncertain light. In
illustrating the manners of the peasantry of Nithsdale and
Galloway, it becomes a duty to give some account of
their popular superstitions; and of these the native
Fairies and Witches are the most singular. They possess
a feature of individuality distinct from those of other
nations, and congenial to the peculiar character of the
people. On this subject the reader will, doubtless, prefer
the testimony of oral tradition to the more doubtful
authority of antiquarian lore, and black-letter research.

There are few old people who have not a powerful
belief in the influence and dominion of fairies ; few who
do not believe they have heard them on their midnight
excursions, or talked with them amongst their woods and
their knowes, in the familiarity of friendship. So general
was the superstition, that priestly caution deemed it
necessary to interpose its religious authority to forbid
man's intercourse with these " *light infantry of Satan !* "

They were small of stature, exquisitely shaped and proportioned ;—of a fair complexion, with long fleeces of yellow hair flowing over their shoulders, and tucked above their brows with combs of gold. A mantle of green cloth, inlaid with wild flowers, reached to their middle ;—green pantaloons, buttoned with bobs of silk, and sandals of silver, formed their under dress. On their shoulders hung quivers of adder slough, stored with pernicious arrows ; and bows, fashioned from the rib of a man, buried where *"three Lairds' lands meet,"* tipped with gold, ready bent for warfare, were slung by their sides. Thus accoutred they mounted on steeds, whose hoofs would not print the new plowed land, nor dash the dew from the cup of a hare-bell. They visited the flocks, the folds, the fields of coming grain, and the habitations of man ;—and woe to the mortal whose frailty threw him in their power !—A flight of arrows, tipped with deadly plagues, were poured into his folds ; and nauseous weeds grew up in his pastures ; his coming harvest was blighted with pernicious breath,—and whatever he had no longer prospered. These fatal shafts were formed of the bog reed, pointed with white field flint, and dipped in the dew of hemlock. They were shot into cattle with such magical dexterity that the smallest aperture could not be discovered, but by those deeply skilled in Fairy warfare, and in the cure of elf-shooting. Cordials and potent charms are applied ; the

burning arrow is extracted, and instant recovery ensues.
The fairies seem to have been much attached to particular places.   A green hill ;—an opening in a wood ;
—a burn just freeing itself from the uplands, were kept
sacred for revelry and festival.   The Ward-law, an ever
green hill in Dalswinton Barony, was, in olden days, a
noted Fairy tryste.   But the Fairy ring being converted
into a pulpit, in the times of persecution, proscribed the
revelry of unchristened feet.   Lamentations of no earthly voices were heard for years around this beloved hill.
In their festivals they had the choicest earthly cheer ;
nor do they seem to have repelled the intrusion of man,
but invited him to partake of their enjoyments.   A young
man of Nithsdale, being on a love intrigue, was enchanted
with wild and delightful music, and the sound of mingled
voices, more charming than aught that mortal breath
could utter.   With a romantic daring, peculiar to a
Scottish lover, he followed the sound, and discovered
the Fairy banquet :—A green table, with feet of gold,
was placed across a small rivulet, and richly furnished
with pure bread and wines of sweetest flavour.   Their
minstrelsy was raised from small reeds, and stalks of
corn :—he was invited to partake in the dance, and presented with a cup of wine.   He was allowed to depart,
and was ever after endowed with the second sight.   He
boasted of having seen and conversed with several of
his earthly acquaintances whom the Fairies had taken

and admitted as brothers! Mankind, measuring the minds of others by their own enjoyments, have marked out set times of festivity to the Fairies. At the first approach of summer is held the " *Fairy Rade;*"—and their merry minstrelsy, with the tinkling of their horses' housings, and the hubbub of voices, have kept the peasantry in the Scottish villages awake on the first night of summer. They placed branches of rowan tree over their doors, and gazed on the Fairy procession safely from below the charm-proof twig. This march was described to the Editor, with the artless simplicity of sure belief, by an old woman of Nithsdale :—" I' the night afore Roodsmass, I had trysted wi' a neeber lass, a Scots mile frae hame, to talk anent buying braws i' the fair :—we had nae sutten lang aneath the haw-buss, till we heard the loud laugh o' fowk riding, wi' the jingling o' bridles, an' the clanking o' hoofs. We banged up, thinking they wad ryde owre us :—we kent nae but it was drunken fowk riding to the fair, i' the fore night. We glowred roun' and roun', an' sune saw it was the *Fairie fowks Rade.* We cowered down till they passed by. A leam o' light was dancing owre them, mair bonnie than moonshine : they were a wee, wee fowk, wi' green scarfs on, but * ane that rade foremost, and that ane was a gude deal langer than the lave, wi' bonnie lang hair bun' about

---

* *But ane*—except one.

wi' a strap, whilk glented lyke stars.   They rade on braw
wee whyte naigs, wi' unco lang swooping tails, an' manes
hung wi' whustles that the win' played on.   This, an'
their tongues whan they sang, was like the soun' of a far
awa' Psalm.   Marion an' me was in a brade lea fiel'
whare they cam by us, a high hedge o' hawtrees keepit
them frae gaun through Johnnie Corrie's corn :—but
they lap a' owre't like sparrows, an' gallop't into a green
knowe beyont it.   We gade i' the morning to look at
the tredded corn, but the fient a hoof mark was there
nor a blade broken."

In the solitary instances of their intercourse with mankind there is a benevolence of character, or a cruelty of
disposition, which brings them down to be measured by
a mortal standard.   In all these presiding spirits there is
a vein of earthly grossness, which marks them Beings
created by human invention.

It is reckoned by the Scottish peasantry "*Unco sonsie*"
to live in familiar and social terms with them.   They
will borrow or lend ; and it is counted *uncanny* to refuse
a Fairy request.   A woman of Auchencreath, in Nithsdale was one day sifting meal warm from the mill : a
little, cleanly-arrayed, beautiful woman, came to her,
holding out a basin of antique workmanship, requesting
her courteously to fill it with her new meal.   Her de-
mand was cheerfully complied with.   In a week the
comely little dame returned with the borrowed meal.

She breathed over it, setting it down basin and all, saying aloud, "*be never toom.*" The gude-wife lived to a
goodly age, without ever seeing the bottom of her blessed
basin. When an injury was unwittingly done them they
forgave it, and asked for amends like other creatures.

A woman, who lived in the ancient burgh of Loch-
maben, was returning late one evening to her home from
a gossipping. A little, lovely boy, dressed in green,
came to her, saying—"*Coupe yere dish-water farther frae
yere door-step, it pits out our fire!*" This request was complied with, and plenty abode in the good woman's house
all her days.

There are chosen fields of Fairy revelry, which it is
reckoned *unsonsie* to plow, or to reap. Old thorn trees,
in the middle of a field, are deemed the rallying trystes
of Fairies, and are preserved with scrupulous care. Two
lads were opening with the plow one of these fields, and
one of them had described a circle around the Fairy
thorn, which was not to be plowed. They were surprised, when, on ending the furrow, a green table was placed
there, heaped with the choicest cheese, bread and
wine. He who marked out the thorn, sat down without
hesitation, eating and drinking heartily, saying, "*fair fa'
the hands whilk gie.*" His fellow-servant lashed his steeds,
refusing to partake. The courteous plow-man " thrave,"
said my informer, " like a breckan, and was a proverb for

2 G

wisdom, and an oracle of local rural knowledge ever after !"

Their love of mortal commerce prompted them to have their children suckled at earthly breasts. The favoured nurse was chosen from healthful, ruddy complexioned beauty ; one every way approved of by mortal eyes. A fine young woman of Nithsdale, when first made a mother, was sitting singing and rocking her child, when a pretty lady came into her cottage, covered with a Fairy mantle. She carried a beautiful child in her arms, swaddled in green silk : " *Gie my bonnie thing a suck,*" said the Fairy. The young woman, conscious to whom the child belong-ed, took it kindly in her arms, and laid it to her breast. The lady instantly disappeared, saying, " *Nurse kin', an' ne'er want !*" The young mother nurtured the two babes, and was astonished whenever she awoke at finding the richest suits of apparel for both children, with meat of most delicious flavour. This food tasted, says tradition, like loaf mixed with wine and honey. It possessed more miraculous properties than the wilderness manna, preserv-ing its relish even over the seventh day. On the approach of summer the Fairy lady came to see her child. It bound-ed with joy when it beheld her. She was much delighted with its freshness and activity ; taking it in her arms, she bade the nurse follow. Passing through some scroggy woods, skirting the side of a beautiful green hill, they walked mid-way up. On its sunward slope a door opened, disclosing a beauteous porch, which they entered, and the turf closed behind them. The Fairy dropped three drops of a precious dew on the nurse's left eye-lid, and they entered a land of most pleasant and abundant promise. It was watered with fine looping rivulets, and yellow with corn; the fairest trees enclosed its fields, laden with fruit, which dropped honey. The nurse was rewarded with finest webs of cloth, and food of ever-during substance. Boxes of salves, for restoring mortal health, and curing mortal wounds and infirmities, were bestowed on her, with a promise of never needing. The Fairy dropt a green dew over her right eye, and bade her look. She beheld many of her lost friends and acquaintances doing menial drudgery, reaping the corn and gathering the fruits. This, said she, is the punishment of evil deeds ! The Fairy passed her hand over her eye, and restored its mortal faculties. She was conducted to the porch, but had the address to secure the heavenly salve. She lived, and enjoyed the gift of discerning the earth-visiting spirits, till she was the mother of many children; but happening to meet the Fairy lady, who gave her the child, she attempted to shake hands with her—"What ee d'ye see me wi," whispered she? "Wi' them baith," said the . dame. She breathed on her eyes, and even the power of the box failed to restore their gifts again !

Had the Fairies of the Scottish Lowlands always cherished mankind with deeds of hospitality such as this,

their name and power had ranked high among the supernatural beings who preside over the fate of luckless
mortals ; but their attachments were mingled with base
and unworthy passions, and fitted them for breaking
through the moral obligations of society.   Hence they
began to covet the sons and daughters of men, and pro-
moted with their elfin power, this base attachment.   The
young men of greatest promise, and the fair maids of
most comely virtue, and of rarest personal beauty, were
naturally enough the objects selected by them for the
gratification of these amorous desires.

But these gallantly courteous, and loving elves, did
not confine themselves to unwedded paramours, but
coveted their neighbours' wives ; nor did they meanly
steal their choice, after a vulgar or ordinary manner, but
laid ambushes, and formed stratagems beyond the reach
of earthly conception.

Alexander Harg, a cottar, in the parish of New-Abbey,
had courted and married a pretty girl, whom the Fairies
had long attempted to seduce from this world of love
and wedlock.   A few nights after his marriage, he was
standing with a *halve* net, awaiting the approach of the tide.
Two old vessels, stranded on the rocks, were visible at
mid-water mark, and were reckoned occasional haunts of
the Fairies when crossing the mouth of the Nith.   In
one of these wrecks a loud noise was heard as of car-
penters at work; a hollow voice cried from the other—

"*Ho, what'r ye doing!*" "*I'm making a wyfe to Sandy Harg!*" replied a voice, in no mortal accent. The husband, astonished and terrified, throws down his net, hastens home, shuts up every avenue of entrance, and folds his young spouse in his arms. At midnight a gentle rap comes to the door, with a most courteous three times touch. The young dame starts to get up; the husband holds her in forbidden silence, and kindly clasps. A foot is heard to depart, and instantly the cattle low and bellow, ramping as if pulling up their stakes. He clasps his wife more close to his bosom, regardless of her entreaties. The horses, with most frightful neighs, prance, snort, and bound, as if in the midst of flame. She speaks, cries, entreats, struggles: he will not move, speak, nor quit her. The noise and tumult increases, but with the morning's coming it dies away. The husband leaps up with the dawn, and hurries out to view his premises. A piece of moss oak, fashioned to the shape and size of his wife, meets his eye, reared against his garden dyke, and he burns this devilish effigy.

Tradition extends the fairy power to heights which may be deemed encroaching on the prerogative of heaven. The moulding of bodies from wood into the features and proportions of the human form is skilful, and proclaims their power in sculpture; but clothing these in flesh and blood, and breathing into their nostrils

the breath of life, is an emanation from God, and must
be of Divine permission.

For the stealing of handsome and lovely children they
are far famed, and held in great awe.   But their pernicious breath has such power of transformation, that it
is equally dreaded.   The way to cure a breath-blasted
child is worthy of notice.   When the mother's vigilance
hinders the Fairies from carrying her child away, or
changing it, the touch of Fairy hands and their unearthly
breath make it wither away in every limb and lineament,
like a blighted ear of corn, saving the countenance,
which unchangeably retains the sacred stamp of divinity.
The child is undressed and laid out in unbleached linen
new from the loom.   Water is brought from a *blessed
well*, in the utmost silence, before sunrise, in a pitcher
never before wet; in which the child is washed, and its
clothes dipped by the fingers of a virgin.   Its limbs, on
the third morning's experiment, plump up, and all its
former vigour returns.

But matron knowledge has frequently triumphed over
these subtle thieves by daring experiments and desperate
charms.   A beautiful child, of Caerlaverock, in Nithsdale,
on the second day of its birth, and before its baptism,
was changed, none knew how, for an antiquated elf of
hideous aspect.   It kept the family awake with its
nightly yells; biting the mother's breasts, and would
neither be cradled or nursed.   The mother, obliged to

be from home, left it in charge to the servant-girl. The poor lass was sitting bemoaning herself,—'Wer't nae for thy girning face I would knock the big, winnow the corn, and grun the meal!"—"Lowse the cradle band," quoth the Elf, "and tent the neighbours, an' I'll work yere wark." Up started the elf, the wind arose, the corn was chaffed, the outlyers were foddered, the hand mill moved around, as by instinct, and the *knocking mell* did its work with amazing rapidity. The lass, and her elfin servant, rested and diverted themselves, till, on the mistress's approach, it was restored to the cradle, and began to yell anew. The girl took the first opportunity of slyly telling her mistress the adventure. "*What'll we do wi' the wee diel?*" said she. "I'll wirk it a pirn," replied the lass. At the middle hour of night the chimney top was covered up, and every inlet barred and closed. The embers were blown up until glowing hot. and the maid, undressing the elf, tossed it on the fire, It uttered the wildest and most piercing yells, and, in a moment, the Fairies were heard moaning at every wonted avenue, and rattling at the window boards, at the chimney head, and at the door, "In the name o' God bring back the bairn," cried the lass. The window flew up; the earthly child was laid unharmed on the mother's lap, while its grisly substitute flew up the chimney with a loud laugh.

It was the precaution once in families, when a pretty

child was born, to consecrate it to God, and sue for its protection by "taking the Beuk," and other acts of prayer and devotion.

There is an old Scotch adage—

" Whare the scythe cuts and the sock rives
Hae done wi' *fairies* an' *bee-bykes !"*

The land once ripped by the plowshare, or the sward once passed over by the scythe proclaimed the banishment of the Fairies from holding residence there ever after. The quick progress of Lowland agriculture will completely overthrow their empire ; none now are seen, save solitary and dejected fugitives, ruminating among the ruins of their fallen kingdom !

The "*Fairy Fareweel*," is a circumstance that happened about twenty years ago, and is well remembered. The sun was setting on a fine summer's evening, and the peasantry were returning from labour, when, on the side of a green hill, appeared a procession of thousands of apparently little boys, habited in mantles of green, freckled with light. One, taller than the rest, ran before them, and seemed to enter the hill, and again appeared at its summit. This was repeated three times, and all vanished. The peasantry, who beheld it, called it " *The Fareweel o' the Fairies to the Burrow hill !"*

APPENDIX (G) p. 110.

PARTICULARS OF THE ESCAPE OF LORD NITHSDALE FROM THE TOWER.

The following account of the Earl of Nithsdale's escape, written by his Lady, who contrived and effected it, is so full of interest that, as it must suffer materially by curtailment, the Editor has thought proper to give it entire. It exhibits a memorable instance of that heroic intrepidity to which the female heart can rouse itself on trying occasions when man, notwithstanding his boasted superiority, is but too apt to give way to panic and despair. The tenderness of conjugal affection, and the thousand apprehensions and anxieties that beset it in adversity, the long pressure of misfortune, and the dread of impending calamity, tend uniformly to overwhelm the spirits, and distract the mind from any settled purpose; but it is possible that those sentiments may be absorbed in a more energetic feeling, in a courage sustained by the conflicting influence of hope and desperation. Yet even thus prepared the mind may be inadequate to the attainment of a long and perilous enterprise, and in the present case we have the testimony of Lady Nithsdale herself that she would have sunk at the prospect of so many and such fearful obstacles had she not relied with firmness on the aid of Providence. The detail of her narrative will shew how greatly this reliance contributed

2 H

to strengthen and regulate the tone of her resolution not only in every vicissitude of expectation and disappointment, but in what is more trying than either, the sickening intervals of suspense and doubt.

The original manuscript, from which the present copy has been carefully transcribed, is entitled " A Letter from the Countess of Nithsdale to her sister Lady Lucy Herbert, Abbess of the Augustine Nuns at Bruges, containing a circumstantial account of the Earl of Nithisdale's escape from the Tower," dated " Palais Royal de Rome, 16th April 1718," and signed " Winifred Nithisdale." The letter is now at Terreagles, in the possession of Constable Maxwell, Esq., a descendant of the noble House of Nithsdale, for whose politeness and liberality in allowing a transcription of the present copy the Editor is sincerely grateful.

As a proof of the interest which the public took in this extraordinary adventure, the following memorandum may be given. "William Maxwell, Earl of Nithsdale, made his escape from the Tower, Feb. 23, 1715, dressed in a woman's cloak and hood, which were for some time after called *Nithsdales.*"

" DEAR SISTER,
" My Lord's escape is now such an old story that I have almost forgotten it ; but, since you desire me to give

a circumstantial account of it, I will endeavour to recal it to my memory, and be as exact in the narration as I possibly can ; for I owe you too many obligations to refuse you any thing that lies in my power to do.

"I think I owe myself the justice to set out with the motives which influenced me to undertake so hazardous an attempt, which I despaired of thoroughly accomplishing, foreseeing a thousand obstacles which never could be surmounted but by the most particular interposition of Divine Providence. I confided in the Almighty God, and trusted that he would not abandon me, even when all human succours failed me.

"I first came to London upon hearing that my Lord was committed to the Tower. I was at the same time informed, that he had expressed the greatest anxiety to see me, having, as he afterwards told me, nobody to console him till I arrived. I rode to Newcastle, and from thence took the stage to York. When I arrived there, the snow was so deep, that the stage could not set out for London. The season was so severe, and the roads so extremely bad, that the post itself was stopt : however, I took horses, and rode to London through the snow, which was generally above the horse's girth, and arrived safe and sound without any accident.

"On my arrival, I went immediately to make what interest I could among those who were in place. No one gave me any hopes ; but all, to the contrary, assured me, that although some of the prisoners were to be pardoned, yet my Lord would certainly not be of the number. When I inquired into the reason of this distinction, I could obtain no other answer, than that they would not flatter me : but I soon perceived the reasons which they declined alleging to me. A Roman Catholic, upon the frontiers of Scotland, who headed a very considerable party ; a man whose family had always signalized itself by its loyalty to the Royal House of Stuart, and who was the only support of the Catholics against the inveteracy of the Whigs, who were very numerous in that part of Scotland, would become an agreeable sacrifice to the opposite party. They still retained a lively remembrance of his grandfather, who defended his own castle of Caerlaverock to the very last extremity, and surrendered it up only by the express command of his Royal Master. Now having his grandson in their power, they were determined not to let him escape from their hands.

" Upon this I formed the resolution to attempt his escape, but opened my intentions to nobody but to my dear Evans. In order to concert measures, I strongly solicited to be permitted to see my Lord, which they refused to grant me unless I would remain confined with him in the Tower. This I would not submit to, and alleged for excuse, that my health would not permit me to undergo the confinement. The real reason of my refusal was, not to put it out of my power to accomplish

my design : however, by bribing the guards, I often contrived to see my Lord, till the day upon which the
prisoners were condemned ; after that we were allowed
for the last week to see and take our leave of them.

"By the help of Evans, I had prepared every thing
necessary to disguise my Lord, but had the utmost difficulty to prevail upon him to make use of them : however,
I at length succeeded by the help of Almighty God.

"On the 22d February, which fell on a Thursday, our
petition was to be presented to the House of Lords, the
purport of which was, to entreat the Lords to intercede
with his Majesty to pardon the prisoners. We were, however, disappointed the day before the petition was to be
presented ; for the Duke of St. Albans, who had promised
my Lady Derwentwater to present it, when it came to
the point failed in his word : however, as she was the only
English Countess concerned, it was incumbent upon her
to have it presented. We had one day left before the
execution, and the Duke still promised to present the
petition ; but, for fear he should fail, I engaged the Duke
of Montrose, to secure its being done by the one or the
other. I then went in company of most of the ladies of
quality, who were then in town, to solicit the interest of
the Lords as they were going to the House. They all
behaved to me with great civility, but particularly my
Lord Pembroke, who, though he desired me not to speak
to him, yet promised to employ his interest in our favour,

and honourably kept his word ; for he spoke in the House
very strongly in our behalf. The subject of the debate
was, Whether the King had the power to pardon those
who had been condemned by Parliament ? And it was
chiefly owing to Lord Pembroke's speech that it passed
in the affirmative ; however, one of the Lords stood up
and said, that the House would only intercede for those
of the prisoners who should approve themselves worthy
of their intercession, but not for all of them indiscrimin-
ately. This salvo quite blasted all my hopes, for I was
assured it aimed at the exclusion of those who should
refuse to subscribe to the petition, which was a thing I
knew my Lord would never submit to ; nor, in fact,
could I wish to preserve his life on such terms.

"As the motion had passed generally, I thought I
could draw some advantage in favour of my design.
Accordingly, I immediately left the House of Lords,
and hastened to the Tower, where, affecting an air of joy
and satisfaction, I told all the guards I passed by, that I
came to bring joyful tidings to the prisoners. I desired
them to lay aside their fears, for the petition had passed
the House in their favour. I then gave them some
money to drink to the Lords and his Majesty, though it
was but trifling ; for I thought that, if I were too liberal
on the occasion, they might suspect my designs, and that
giving them something would gain their good humour
and services for the next day, which was the eve of the
execution.

" The next morning I could not go to the Tower, having so many things in my hands to put in readiness ; but in the evening, when all was ready, I sent for Mrs. Mills, with whom I lodged, and acquainted her with my design of attempting my Lord's escape, as there was no prospect of his being pardoned ; and this was the last night before the execution. I told her, that I had every thing in readiness, and that I trusted she would not refuse to accompany me, that my Lord might pass for her. I pressed her to come immediately, as we had no time to lose. At the same time I sent for Mrs. Morgan, then usually known by the name of Hilton, to whose acquaintance my dear Evans has introduced me, which I looked upon as a very singular happiness. I immediately communicated my resolution to her. She was of a very tall and slender make ; so I begged her to put under her own riding-hood, one that I prepared for Mrs. Mills, as she was to lend her's to my Lord, that, in coming out, he might be taken for her. Mrs. Mills was then with child ; so that she was not only of the same height, but nearly the same size as my Lord. When we were in the coach, I never ceased talking, that they might have no leisure to reflect. Their surprise and astonishment when I first opened my design to them, had made them consent, without ever thinking of the consequences. On our arrival at the Tower, the first I introduced was Mrs. Morgan ; for I was only allowed to take in one at a time.

She brought in the clothes that were to serve Mrs. Mills, when she left her own behind her.   When Mrs. Morgan had taken off what she had brought for my purpose, I conducted her back to the stair-case ; and, in going, I begged her to send me in my maid to dress me ; that I was afraid of being too late to present my last petition that night, if she did not come immediately.   I despatched her safe, and went partly down stairs to meet Mrs. Mills, who had the precaution to hold her handkerchief to her face, as was very natural for a woman to do when she was going to bid her last farewell to a friend on the eve of his execution.   I had, indeed, desired her to do it, that my Lord might go out in the same manner. Her eyebrows were rather inclined to be sandy, and my Lord's were dark, and very thick : however, I had prepared some paint of the colour of hers to disguise his with.   I also bought an artificial head-dress of the same coloured hair as hers ; and I painted his face with white and his cheeks with rouge, to hide his long beard, which he had not. had time to shave.   All this provision I had before left in the Tower.   The poor guards, whom my slight liberality the day before had endeared me to, let me go quietly with my company, and were not so strictly on the watch as they usually had been ; and the more so, as they were persuaded, from what I had told them the day before, that the prisoners would obtain their pardon. I made Mrs. Mills take off her own hood, and put on that which I had brought for her. I then took her by the hand, and led her out of my Lord's chamber; and, in passing through the next room, in which there were several people, with all the concern imaginable, I said, my dear Mrs. Catharine, go in all haste, and send me my waiting-maid : she certainly cannot reflect how late it is : she forgets that I am to present a petition to-night ; and, if I let slip this opportunity, I am undone ; for to-morrow will be too late. Hasten her as much as possible ; for I shall be on thorns till she comes. Every body in the room, who were chiefly the guards' wives and daughters, seemed to compassionate me exceedingly, and the centinel officiously opened the door. When I had seen her out, I returned back to my Lord, and finished dressing him. I had taken care that Mrs. Mills did not go out crying as she came in, that my Lord might the better pass for the lady who came in crying and afflicted; and the more so, because he had the same dress she wore. When I had almost finished dressing my Lord in all my petticoats, excepting one, I perceived that it was growing dark, and was afraid that the light of the candles might betray us ; so I resolved to set off. I went out, leading him by the hand ; and he held his handkerchief to his eyes. I spoke to him in the most piteous and afflicted tone of voice, bewailing bitterly the negligence of Evans, who had ruined me by her delay. Then said I, My dear Mrs. Betty, for the love of God, run quickly and bring

her with you.   You know my lodging ; and, if ever you
made dispatch in your life, do it at present : I am almost
distracted with this disappointment.   The guards opened
the doors, and I went down stairs with him, still conjuring
him to make all possible dispatch.   As soon as he had
cleared the door, I made him walk before me, for fear
the centinel should take notice of his walk ; but I still
continued to press him to make all the dispatch he possibly could.   At the bottom of the stairs I met my dear
Evans, into whose hands I confided him.   I had before
engaged Mr. Mills to be in readiness before the Tower to
conduct him to some place of safety, in case we succeeded.
He looked upon the affair so very improbable to succeed,
that his astonishment, when he saw us, threw him into
such consternation, that he was almost out of himself;
which Evans perceiving, with the greatest presence of
mind, without telling him any thing, lest he should mis-
trust them, conducted him to some of her own friends,
on whom she could rely, and so secured him, without
which we should have been undone.   When she had
conducted him, and left him with them, she returned to
find Mr. Mills, who by this time had recovered himself
from his astonishment.   They went home together ; and,
having found a place of security, they conducted him to
it.

" In the mean while, as I had pretended to have sent
the young lady on a message, I was obliged to return

up stairs, and go back to my Lord's room, in the same feigned anxiety of being too late ; so that every body seemed sincerely to sympathise with my distress. When I was in the room, I talked to him as if he had been really present, and answered my own questions in my Lord's voice as nearly as I could imitate it. I walked up and down, as if we were conversing together, till I thought they had time enough thoroughly to clear themselves of the guards. I then thought proper to make off also. I opened the door, and stood half in it, that those in the outward chamber might hear what I said ; but held it so close, that they could not look in. I bid my Lord a formal farewell for that night ; and added, that something more than usual must have happened to make Evans negligent on this important occasion, who had always been so punctual in the smallest trifles : that I saw no other remedy than to go in person : that, if the Tower were still open when I finished my business, I would return that night ; but that he might be assured I would be with him as early in the morning as I could gain admittance into the Tower ; and I flattered myself I should bring favourable news. Then, before I shut the door, I pulled through the string of the latch, so that it could only be opened on the inside. I then shut it with some degree of force, that I might be sure of its being well shut. I said to the servant as I passed by, who was ignorant of the whole transaction, that he need not carry in candles to his master till my Lord sent for him, as he desired to finish some prayers first. I went down stairs, and called a coach. As there were several on the stand, I drove home to my lodgings, where poor Mr. Mackenzie had been waiting to carry the petition, in case my attempt had failed. I told him there was no need of any petition, as my Lord was safe out of the Tower, and out of the hands of his enemies, as I hoped; but that I did not know where he was.

"I discharged the coach, and sent for a sedan chair, and went to the Duchess of Buccleugh, who expected me about that time, as I had begged of her to present the petition for me, having taken my precautions against all events, and asked if she were at home; and they answered, that she expected me, and had another Duchess with her. I refused to go up stairs, as she had company with her, and I was not in a condition to see any other company. I begged to be shown into a chamber below stairs, and that they would have the goodness to send her Grace's maid to me, having something to say to her. I had discharged the chair, lest I might be pursued and watched. When the maid came in, I desired her to present my most humble respects to her Grace, who they told me had company with her, and to acquaint her that this was my only reason for not coming up stairs. I also charged her with my sincerest thanks for her kind offer to accompany me when I went to present my petition.

I added, that she might spare herself any further trouble, as it was now judged more advisable to present one general petition in the name of all : however, that I should never be unmindful of my particular obligations to her Grace, which I would return very soon to acknowledge in person.

"I then desired one of the servants to call a chair, and I went to the Duchess of Montrose, who had always borne a part in my distresses. When I arrived, she left her company to deny herself, not being able to see me under the affliction which she judged me to be in. By mistake, however, I was admitted ; so there was no remedy. She came to me ; and, as my heart was in an ecstasy of joy, I expressed it in my countenance as she entered the room. I ran up to her in the transport of my joy. She appeared to be extremely shocked and frighted ; and has since confessed to me, that she apprehended my trouble had thrown me. out of myself, till I communicated my happiness to her. She then advised me to retire to some place of security : for that the King was highly displeased, and even enraged at the petition that I had presented to him, and had complained of it severely. I sent for another chair ; for I always discharged them immediately, lest I might be pursued. Her Grace said she would go to court, to see how the news of my Lord's escape was received. When the news was brought to the King, he flew into an excess of passion, and said he was betrayed ; for it could not have been done without some confederacy.   He instantly dispatched two persons to the Tower, to see that the other prisoners were well secured, lest they should follow the example.   Some threw the blame upon one, some upon another ; the Duchess was the only one at the court who knew it.

"When I left the Duchess, I went to a house which Evans had found out for me, and where she promised to acquaint me where my Lord was.   She got thither some few minutes after me, and told me that, when she had seen him secure, she went in search of Mr. Mills, who, by the time, had recovered himself from his astonishment ; that he had returned to her house, where she had found him ; and that he had removed my Lord from the first place, where she had desired him to wait, to the house of a poor woman, directly opposite to the guard-house.   She had but one small room up one pair of stairs, and a very small bed in it.   We threw ourselves upon the bed, that we might not be heard walking up and down.   She left us a bottle of wine and some bread, and Mrs. Mills brought us some more in her pocket the next day.   We subsisted on this provision from Thursday till Saturday night, when Mrs. Mills came and conducted my Lord to the Venetian Ambassador.   We did not communicate the affair to his Excellency ; but one of his servants concealed him in his own room till Wednesday, on which day the Ambassador's coach and six was to go down to Dover to meet his brother. My Lord put on a livery, and went down in the retinue, without the least suspicion, to Dover, where Mr. Mitchell (which was the name of the Ambassador's servant) hired a small vessel, and immediately set sail for Calais. The passage was so remarkably short, that the captain threw out this reflection, that the wind could not have served better if his passengers had been flying for their lives, little thinking it to be really the case. Mr. Mitchell might have easily returned without being suspected of having been concerned in my Lord's escape ; but my Lord seemed inclined to have him continue with him, which he did, and has at present a good place under our young master.

" This is as exact and as full an account of this affair and of the persons concerned in it, as I could possibly give you, to the best of my memory, and you may rely on the truth of it. I am, with the strongest attachment, my Dear Sister, your's most affectionately,

WINIFRED NITHISDALE."

APPENDIX (H) p. 172.

ACCOUNT OF BILLIE BLIN'.

This is another name for the Scotch *Brownies*, a class of solitary beings, living in the hollows of trees, and re-

cesses of old ruinous castles.   They are described as
being small of stature, covered wtth short curly hair, with
brown matted locks, and a brown mantle which reached
to the knee, with a hood of the same colour.   They were
particularly attached to families eminent for their ancestry and virtue ; and have lived, according to tradition's
" undoubted mouth," for several hundreds of years in the
same family, doing the drudgery of a menial servant.
But though very trusty servants, they were somewhat coy
in their manner of doing their work :—when the *threaves*
of corn were counted out they remained unthrashen ; at
other times, however great the quantity, it was finished
by the crowing of the first cock.   *Mellers* of corn would
be dried, ground, and sifted, with such exquisite nicety,
that the finest flour of the meal could not be found
strewed or lost.   The Brownie would then come into the
farm-hall, and stretch itself out by the chimney, sweaty,
dusty and fatigued.   It would take up the *pluff,* (a piece
of bored bour-tree for blowing up the fire) and, stirring
out the red embers, turn itself till it was rested and dried.
A choice bowl of sweet cream, with combs of honey, was
set in an accessible place :—this was given as its hire ;
and it was willing to be bribed, though none durst avow
the intention of the gift.   When offered meat or drink,
the Brownie instantly departed, bewailing and lamenting
itself, as if unwilling to leave a place so long its habita-
tion, from which nothing but the superior power of fate

could sever it. A thrifty good wife, having made a web of linsey-woolsey, sewed a well-lined mantle and a comfortable hood for her trusty Brownie. She laid it down in one of his favourite haunts, and cried to him to array himself. Being commissioned by the gods to relieve mankind under the drudgery of original sin, he was forbidden to accept of wages or bribes. He instantly departed, bemoaning himself in a rhyme, which tradition has faithfully preserved :

"A new mantle, and a new hood !—
Poor Brownie ! ye'll ne'er do mair gude."

The prosperity of the family seemed to depend on them, and was at their disposal. A place, called Liethin Hall, in Dumfries-shire, was the hereditary dwelling of a noted Brownie. He had lived there, as he once communicated, in confidence, to an old woman, for three hundred years. He appeared only once to every new master, and indeed seldom shewed more than his hand to any one. On the decease of a beloved master, he was heard to make moan, and would not partake of his wonted delicacies for many days. The heir of the land arrived from foreign parts and took possession of his father's inheritance. The faithful Brownie shewed himself and proffered homage. The spruce Laird was offended to see such a famine-faced, wrinkled domestic, and ordered him meat and drink, with a new suit of clean

2 K

livery.   The Brownie departed, repeating loud and frequently these ruin-boding lines—

> " Ca', cuttie, ca !
> A' the luck o' Liethin Ha'
> Gangs wi' me to Bodsbeck Ha."

Liethin Ha' was, in a few years, in ruins, and "bonnie
Bodsbeck" flourished under the luck-bringing patronage
of the Brownie.

They possessed all the adventurous and chivalrous
gallantry of crusading knighthood, but in devotion to the
ladies they left Errantry itself far behind.   Their services
were really useful.   In the accidental encounters of their
fair mistresses with noble outlaws in woods, and princes
in disguise,— when the *kind ladies* had nothing to shew
for their courtesy but a comb of gold or a fillet of hair,—
the faithful Brownie restored the noble wooer ; laid the
lovers on their bridal bed, declared their lineage, and re-
conciled all parties.   He followed his dear mistress
through life with the same kindly solicitude ;—for, when
the " mother's trying hour was nigh," with the most
laudable promptitude he environed her with the " cannie
dames," ere the wish for their assistance was half-formed
in her mind.

One of them, in the olden times, lived with Maxwell,
Laird of Dalswinton, doing ten men's work, and keeping
the servants awake at nights with the noisy dirling of its
elfin flail.   The Laird's daughter, says tradition, was the

comeliest dame in all the holms of Nithsdale. To her the Brownie was much attached : he assisted her in love-intrigue, conveying her from her high-tower-chamber to the trysting-thorn in the woods, and back again, with such light heeled celerity, that neither bird, dog, nor servant awoke.

He undressed her for the matrimonial bed, and served her so hand maiden-like that her female attendant had nothing to do, not daring even to finger her mistress's apparel, lest she should provoke the Brownie's resentment. When the pangs of the mother seized his beloved lady, a servant was ordered to fetch the "cannie wife," who lived across the Nith. The night was dark as a December night could be ; and the wind was heavy among the groves of oak. The Brownie, enraged at the loitering serving-man, wrapped himself in his lady's fur-cloak ; and, though the Nith was foaming high-flood, his steed, impelled by supernatural spur and whip, passed it like an arrow. Mounting the dame behind him, he took the deep water back again to the amazement of the worthy woman, who beheld the red waves tumbling around her, yet the steed's foot-locks were dry.—"Ride nae by the auld pool," quo" she, "lest we should meet wi' Brownie."—He replied, "Fear nae, dame, ye've met a' the Brownies ye will meet."—Placing her down at the hall gate, he hastened to the stable, where the servant-lad was just pulling on his boots ; he unbuckled the bridle

from his steed, and gave him a most afflicting drubbing.
—This was about the new-modelling times of the Reformation; and a priest, more zealous than wise, exhorted
the Laird to have this Imp of Heathenism baptized; to
which he, in an evil hour, consented, and the worthy reforming saint concealed himself in the barn, to surprise
the Brownie at his work.   He appeared like a little,
wrinkled, ancient man, and began his nightly moil.   The
priest leapt from his ambush, and dashed the baptismal
water in his face, solemnly repeating the set form of
Christian rite.   The poor Brownie set up a frightful and
agonizing yell, and instantly vanished, never to return.

The Brownie, though of a docile disposition, was not
without its pranks and merriment.   The Abbey-lands, in
the parish of New Abbey, were the residence of a very
sportive one.   He loved to be, betimes, somewhat mischievous.—Two lasses, having made a fine bowlful of
buttered brose, had taken it into the byre to sup, while
it was yet dark.   In the haste of concealment they had
brought but one spoon; so they placed the bowl between
them, and took a spoonful by turns.   "I hae got but three
sups," cried the one, "an' it's a' done!"   "It's a' done,
indeed," cried the other.   "Ha, ha!" laughed a third
voice, "Brownie has gotten the maist o't."   He had
judiciously placed himself between them, and got the
spoon twice for their once.

The Brownie does not seem to have loved the gay and

gaudy attire in which his twin-brothers, the Fairies, arrayed themselves : his chief delight was in the tender delicacies of food. Knuckled cakes, made of meal, warm
from the mill, *haurned* on the decayed embers of the fire,
and smeared with honey, were his favourite hire ; and
they were carefully laid so that he might accidentally
find them.——It is still a common phrase, when a child
gets a little eatable present, "there's a piece wad please
a Brownie." His mantle and hood seemed of perdur-
able materials, and remained undecayed for hundreds of
years. In the articles of nicest housewifery he excelled ;
witched cream that had been churned without success,
when touched by the charm-dispelling fingers of the
Brownie, yielded its yellow treasure. In the morning the
butter would be found neatly washed and beautifully
dressed out ; the kirn and staff well scalded, and placed
in their former situation. They were the noted guardians
of the "kind bees," and the protectors of the dairy, so
that the proverb was almost plucked from Canaan's brow,
of a land flowing with milk and honey. They were, to
all appearance, beings of a very superior race ; invulner-
able to the spells and cantrips of deadly witchcraft and
proof against every thing but baptismal affusion. They
bore neither bows nor shafts like the Fairies, but relied
solely on their own superior endowments. Their love of
women and dainty food, proves them of earthly mixture;
but they conducted themselves in a way worthy of their

celestial origin.   In family economy they were unrivalled;
and the degeneracy of Scottish housewifery may be justly
laid on the baptizing ferocity of their stern reformers,
which banished from the farmer's hearth the noblest
domestic that industry ever held in fee.*

To estimate justly the high character of the Scottish
Peasantry, and to acquire a true relish for the exquisite
beauties of their Doric dialect, it is necessary to live
among them, and to enter into their ideas and feelings.
The Editor, therefore, in closing his account of them,
dares not indulge any sanguine hopes that it will be as
acceptable in his own country as in Scotland.   This
apprehension is discouraging ; but he has the satisfaction
to observe, that much of what he had to say in recom-
mending the Scottish Peasantry to the notice of his
countrymen, has been anticipated by an authority very
generally respected,—the *Edinburgh Review*.   In N°
XXXI., in a critique on Mr. Grahame's *Georgics*, are the
following comprehensive and philosophical observations :
   " The last peculiarity by which Mr. Grahame's poetry

---

* Some features of this story have been already laid before the public by Mr.
Scott.   The Editor hopes, however, that he may venture, without any violation
of modesty, to assert, that the account here given, is in itself original and to him
it appears more complete than that in the *Minstrelsy*.   Should the Reader be
of the same opinion the want of entire novelty will easily be forgiven.

is recommended to us, is one which we hesitate a little
about naming to our English readers :—to be candid with
them, however, it is his great nationality. We do love
him in our hearts, we are afraid, for speaking so affectionately of Scotland. But, independent of this partial
bias, we must say, that the exquisitely correct pictures
which he has drawn of Scottish rustics, and of Scottish
rustic scenery, have a merit, which even English critics
would not think we had overrated if they were as well
qualified as we are to judge of their fidelity. We will
add, too, in spite of the imputations to which it may
expose us, that the rustics of Scotland are a far more
interesting race, and far fitter subjects for poetry
than their brethern of the same condition in the South.
They are much more thoughtful, pious, and intelligent ;
have more delicacy in their affections, and more reflecting,
patient and serious kindness in their natures. To say all
in a word, they are far less *brutish* than the great body of
the English peasantry. At the same time, from being
poorer and more lonely, their characters and way of life
are more truly simple, while the very want of comfort
and accommodation with which they are sometimes surrounded, holds more of the antique age, and connects
them more closely with those primitive times, with the
customs and even the history of which they are still so
generally familiar. The Scottish landscape, too, we
must be pardoned for thinking, is better suited for poetical

purposes than the prevailing scenery of England. Its
great extent and openness—the slight shade of dreariness
that is commonly thrown over both its beauty and sublimity—and the air of wildness and antiquity which it
derives from its rocky hills and unploughed valleys,—
possess a charm both to the natives and to strangers, that
leads far more readily to poetical associations than the
fertile fields and snug villages of the South."

The Editor will close this volume with some account
of the Life and Writings of JOHN LOWE, one of the most
distinguished of the Galloway bards.

BRIEF MEMOIR

OF THE

LIFE OF JOHN LOWE,
Author of " Mary's Dream."

By the Reverend *WILLIAM GILLESPIE,*
MINISTER OF KELLS PARISH, IN GALLOWAY.

As no pathetic ballad was ever more popular in this country than " MARY'S DREAM," it is presumed that some account of its author, (who was a native of Galloway,) will not be considered an intrusion in the present Collection. The authenticity of the memoir will not be doubted, when it is known that the gentleman who communicated it is minister of the parish in which Lowe was born, and that his father was one of the poet's best friends, and most intimate correspondents. The history of the latter part of his life, which he spent abroad, Mr. Gillespie collects from notices furnished by his own correspondence, and from the communication of the Rev. Mr. M'Conochie (an old and early associate of Lowe's,) transmitted from Virginia, which gives the unfortunate particulars of his death.

If the public sympathize in the interest felt by the Editor on perusing this excellent memoir, their approbation will give a value to the thanks which he here expresses to the gentleman by whom it was communicated.

John Lowe, author of the pathetic and popular ballad " Mary's Dream," was born at Kenmore in Galloway, in the year 1750. His father was gardener to Mr. Gordon of Kenmore, son of that unfortunate nobleman who paid the forfeit of his life and titles for his adherence to the House of Stewart in 1715. Our poet was the eldest of a numerous family, and as the excellent institution of parish schools in Scotland affords, to the humblest of her sons, the opportunity of educating his children, so Lowe was early put to the parish school of Kells, where, under an assiduous and able teacher, he imbibed the rudiments of classical education. He discovered an early ambition of becoming a scholar, but, on leaving school, his father's narrow circumstances did not enable him to assist his son in the further prosecution of his studies. At the age of fourteen he was bound as a weaver to a respectable and industrious tradesman of the name of Heron, father of Robert Heron, author of a History of Scotland, and of several elegant translations from the French language.

He was impelled by " dire necessity," to follow an employment so unsuitable to his genius, for, by the earnings of his labour, he soon afterwards put himself to school under one M'Kay, then schoolmaster of the neighbouring parish of Carsphairn, an eminent teacher of the languages. He employed his evenings in teaching church music, as he possessed a very just ear, sung well, and played with considerable skill on the violin. These qualities, added to a happy temper, and an uncommon flow of animal spirits, made Lowe very acceptable wherever he went, and gained him many friends who assisted him in his education, both with their money and their advice. In these respects, he was eminently indebted to the minister of his native parish, a man as distinguished for the disinterested benevolence of his character, as for his sublime and unaffected piety, and his cheerful and amiable manners.* By these means Lowe was enabled to enter himself as a student in the University of Edinburgh in the year 1771. For this generosity of his friends he is accused of never having afterwards been sufficiently grateful, but while he ceased not to express, in the warmest manner, his obligations to his benefactors, his malignant fortune denied him the means of cancelling them. Even in his best days, prosperity smiled upon him, rather in hope, than in possession, and a dependant man, struggling with difficulties, is frequently obliged to procrastinate the day of payment, to make promises he is unable to fulfil, and to breathe wishes he has no power to realize.

* The late Rev. John Gillespie, Minister of Kells.

In his most juvenile letters we trace the mind of the
poet alive to every change of nature, and vicissitude of
the seasons. "We have had," (says he, in one of his
earliest letters from college,) "a long and severe storm
here, but now we have a very agreeable spring, the time
of the singing of birds is come, and the song of joy is already heard in our land. How sweet now to leave the
noise of the busy world, and with frequent footsteps to
gather health from the gale of the morning! To raise
the soul to heaven with pious ardour, and hail the new-
born day! To bask in the cheerful beams of the sun, the
image of its great original! In short, we are like people
transported in an instant, from the terrible icy shore of
Zembla, where eternal tempests madden, and dreadful
whirlwinds roar amid the frozen mountains,—to the banks
of the Nile, where a lasting verdure clothes the fertile
plains, where wintry blasts, and the storms of dark December, are never known. Pardon a comparison so bold,
but I am enraptured with the agreeable change, and I
dare say you will be so also."

On his return from college, he became tutor in the
family of Mr. M'Ghie, of Aird, an amiable country
gentleman of small fortune, who had several beautiful
daughters. The house of Airds is pleasantly situated on

a rising ground embowered with trees, washed on one side by the Ken, and on the other by the Dee, which here unite in one river under the common name of Dee, though this is but a tributary stream. It is not easy to conceive a situation more favourable to the descriptive Muse ; and here, Lowe, who had previously given some marks of a poetical vein, gave free scope to his genius, and composed many little pieces which he frequently recited to his friends with great enthusiasm. Of these, it is to be regretted that few copies are now to be found, though there are some songs yet sung by the common people (in that district of Galloway called the Glenkens,) which still bear his name. At this period of life, when the mind delights more in description than in sentiment, in pictures of nature than in those of manners, he composed a pretty long pastoral poem entitled a "*Morning Poem*," which is still preserved entire in his own handwriting, and, though written at a time when his taste was but imperfectly formed, is the offspring of a lively imagination and of one who "mused o'er nature with a poet's eye."—He here, likewise, attempted to write a tragedy, the scenes of which he used to read to some of his companions, as he successively composed them ; but as this, the highest effort of human genius, was at that time, and perhaps at any time, above his reach, there is no cause to regret that no part of it is now to be obtained.

He used to invoke his Muse from the top of a pictur-

esque cliff, which rises suddenly over a thick wood on the
banks of the Ken, and commands a varied, beautiful, and
extensive view of the surrounding landscape. He erected
for himself a rural seat on this spot, which is still called
"Lowe's seat," and planted it round with honeysuckles,
woodbines, and other wild shrubs and flowers. Here he
recited aloud his poetic effusions to the invisible inhabitants of the woods and the streams, and here likewise it
was he composed the well-known ballad which makes the
story of his life chiefly interesting to the public. *

> " High on a rock his favorite arbour stood,
> Near Ken's fair bank, amid a verdant wood ;
> Beneath its grateful shade, at ease he lay,
> And view'd the beauties of the rising day ;
> Whilst with mellifluous lays the groves did ring
> He also join'd."
>
> LOWE'S " MORNING."

There was lost at sea, about this time, a gentleman of
the name of Miller, a surgeon, who had been engaged to
MARY, one of the young ladies of Airds, an event which
would long since have been forgotten but for the tender

---

* In a letter, written seven years afterwards from America, to an early friend,
he says—" The beautiful banks of the river Rappehanock, where the town in
which I now reside is situated, with all their luxuriance and fragrance, have
never to me had charms equal to smooth Ken, or murmuring Dee." " Thou
wood of Airds ! balmy retreat of peace, innocence, harmony, and love, with what
raptures do I still reflect on thee ! When were you there, and does my arbour
still remain, or is there now any vestige of my favourite walk ?"

song of "Mary's Dream," which has given to it immortality. It is to be presumed, that our poet was sensibly alive to the misfortunes of a young lady whose sister had inspired him also with the tenderest passion ; and we regret to state that his fidelity to the object of it, though equally worthy of his admiration and his Muse, was but little consistent with the warmth of his feelings, and the earnestness of his professions. But perhaps, he excused himself with the levity of Montaigne, that "love is contrary to its own nature if it be not violent, and that violence is contrary to its own nature if it be constant."

His views were now directed to the Church, and he had spent another session at the University of Edinburgh. Seeing, however, no prospect of a living, and impatient of dependence, he resolved to try his fortune in America, where he fondly hoped his talents would be more highly appreciated, and where he indulged the pious expectation of being better able to assist his aged mother and his other relations at home, for whom he ever expressed the warmest affection. In writing to one of his best friends, he says, " Think not my concealing from you my design of going abroad proceeded from any diffidence of your friendship,—far otherwise.—But for fear of alarming my poor mother : I know how shocking it will be to her, but I hope to have it in my power to be of more service to her there than I could be at home." In the same letter, (dated 13 March, 1773,) he says, " I delivered a discourse this day in the hall with great approbation, both from my professor and fellow-students. As it was the last I shall ever perhaps deliver here, I resolved it should be as good as it was in my power to make it."

He embarked for the new world in the same year, being invited as tutor to the family of a brother of the great Washington, a situation which supplied some hopes to his ambition. He afterwards kept an academy for the education of young gentlemen in Fredricksburgh, Virginia, which succeeded for awhile, as he himself states, " beyond his most sanguine wishes, and to which students resorted from a vast distance." It suffered, however, some interruption by one of those winters of intense frost and deep snows which occur in America ; which, having shut up the town from any communication with the neighbouring country, from which its productions were supplied, compelled him to discharge his boarders, and for some time he was not able to collect them together again. " Often," says he, " have I heard Scotland called a cold place in winter, but never did I experience any thing equal to what I felt here last winter (1784). My thermometer was frequently sunk entirely into the ball, and it was with much difficulty that a fire could then be lighted even in the closest rooms. And when the ice broke away it was the most dreadful sight I ever beheld ; houses, trees, vessels, &c., &c., all moving away together in one common plain of ice on the river Rappehanock, which is close by this town, and the property destroyed is immense beyond description."

Sometime after this Lowe took orders in the Church of England, the then *fashionable* religion of this part of the United States; obtaining a living in that church, and became eminently respectable for his talents, his learning, and his sociable and pleasant manners. He appears to have been so much elated by his good fortune that in some of his letters home he flatters his imagination with the hopes of revisiting his native country in a diplomatic capacity. These were the golden days of Lowe, but an event took place which clouded the meridian of his life, and blasted his happiness for ever.

Two years after he left the shores of Britain he addressed a poem, of considerable length, to her who was the object of his earliest affections, and who seemed still to possess the chief place in his heart.* In this poem he thus breathes his passion—

> " My busy sprite, when balmy sleep descends,
> Flies o'er the deep, and visits all her friends;
> Then, only then, I see my charming dame,
> Ah! must we only meet but in a dream!
> What hindered me when first thy fondest slave,
> My hand to give thee,—as my heart I gave?
> Wedlock itself would need no grave Divine
> To fix his stamp upon such love as mine:
> A love so pure, so tender, and so strong,
> Might last for ages, could we live so long."

---

*This Lady was, after the death of Mr. Lowe, married to a very respectable country gentleman in her native county, and still lives.

And afterwards he adds—

" Fair faces here I meet, and forms divine,
 Enough to shake all constancy but mine."

But notwithstanding the ardour of these professions his constancy was not so much proof, as he imagined, against the temptations to which it was exposed. He became enamoured of a beautiful Virginian lady, and forgot his first love on the banks of the Ken. The young lady, however, refused to listen to his addresses, and he had even the mortification to witness the fair object of his attachment bestowed on a more fortunate and deserving lover. It is singular, that the sister of this very lady became as fondly attached to our poet, as she herself had been indifferent to him, and he allowed himself to be united to her merely, as he states, " from a sentiment of gratitude." But every propitious planet hid its head at the hour which made them one—she proved every thing bad,— and Lowe soon saw in his wife an abandoned woman, regardless of his happiness, and unfaithful even to his bed. Overwhelmed with shame, disappointment and sorrow, he had recourse to the miserable expedient of dissipating at the bottle, the cares and chagrins that preyed upon his heart. Habits of intemperance were thus formed, which, with their wretched attendants, poverty and disease, soon sapped the vigour of a good constitution, and brought him to an untimely grave in the forty-eighth year of his age.*

A letter from Virginia, from an early acquaintance of Lowe's, gives the following particulars respecting his death—That, perceiving his end drawing near, and wishing to die in peace, away from his own wretched walls, he mounted a sorry palfry and rode some distance to the house of a friend. So much was he debilitated that scarcely could he alight in the court and walk into the house. Afterwards, however, he revived a little, and enjoyed some hours of that vivacity which was peculiar to him. But this was but the last faint gleams of a setting sun ; for, on the third day after his arrival at the house of his friend, he breathed his last. He now lies buried near Fredericksburgh, Virginia, under the shade of two palm trees, but not a stone is there on which to write " Mary, weep no more for me !".

The abandoned woman, to whom he had been united, made no enquiries after her husband for more than a month afterwards, when she sent for his horse, which had been previously sold to defray the expenses of his funeral.

---

* From the hasty manner in which I have been compelled to write this Memoir, 1 have not been able to fix the precise time of his death—but, from some circumstances, I am led to place it about 1798, which makes Lowe forty-eight years old when he died.

Such was the tragical end of the author of " Mary's Dream," whose domestic misfortunes " broke a heart already bruised," and terminated a life which was worthy of a better fate.   As a poet, he unquestionably possessed that *vivida vis animi*,—that liveliness of the imagination —that sensibility of the heart which are the inseparable concomitants of poetical genius, or rather, which conspire to form it.   The few fragments which we have of his juvenile poems, imperfect as they are, and made still more so by the inaccurate memories of those from whom they have been chiefly obtained, show a mind capable of still greater efforts, and leave us to regret that he had not cultivated his genius by more frequent exercise.   Much might have been expected from an imagination corrected by maturity of judgment, a taste refined and polished by the perusal of the most finished models, and a diction made more rich and select by unremitted habits of composition.   His " Morning Poem," written at the age of twenty-two, contains some pretty stanzas, of which the following are no unfavourable specimen :—

> " Hail ! to the new born day and cheering light,
> What various beauties charm the ravish'd sight,
> How sweet with early steps, to view the fields,
> And taste the charms which grateful Summer yields,
> With watchful eye, to tread the flowery road,
> And follow nature up to nature's God,—
> On Ken, whose sweet meanders glide away,
> And add new beauties to the rising day ;
> With Dee, whose murmuring music fills the grove,

Where sportive Naiads sing their mutual love ;—
The opening flowers along their borders blow,
And in their bosoms with fresh lustre glow ;
In every wood, the feather'd songsters raise
Their cheerful notes, to sing their Maker's praise.
Aloft in air, the skylark wings his way,
And thrills his notes in sweet melodious lay :
The sooty blackbirds, scatter'd thro' the grove,
Now warble forth their mellow notes of love :
The dark grey thrush, which in the joyful Spring,
My slender pipe had often taught to sing,
On yonder twig sends forth its tuneful voice,
Bids hills be glad, and rising woods rejoice ;
The spreading broom displays its golden hue,
And, nodding, bends beneath the pearly dew ;
The snowy hawthorns, rising here and there,
With grateful fragrance fill the passing air :
Amid their boughs, within each little nest,
The tender passion glows from breast to breast."

The poem called " Lowe's Lines," though very defective in the execution, and, in some of its sentiments, inconsistent both with each other and the passion which it breathes, has likewise some pathetic and beautiful lines, and manifests at once the tenderness of the lover and the imagination of the poet. His letters are well written, and evince a correct and manly understanding, and a warm and benevolent heart. But it was his evil destiny to struggle with dependance, and that time was to be consumed in providing the necessary means of his subsistence, which, in happier circumstances, might have been employed in the indulgence of his genius, the cultivation of his taste, and in twining round his brow the wreath of immortality.

It may not be uninteresting to state that he was very handsome in his person. His figure was active, well proportioned, and rather above the middle size ;—his hair was of an auburn hue, his eyes were blue and penetrating, his nose aquiline, and the whole expression of his countenance open and benevolent. These qualities, united to a fine voice, and lively and insinuating manners, made him a favourite of the fair sex, and he might have secured a handsome independence by marriage if he could have brooked a union in which his heart had no share. He was, however, more susceptible than constant, and one act of infidelity was, by a retributive justice, sufficiently punished by the subsequent misfortunes of his life. His faults, like those of most men of acute sensibility, sprung out of the same soil with his genius and his virtues. It was remarked of him, that he always evinced that manly independence of character, which is the offspring of a superior mind, conscious of its powers ; a quality he shewed even when a boy at school, by a severe beating which he gave to a gentleman's son who was older than himself, and to whom his schoolfellows used to look up with deference ;—and, surely, it becomes us to lean gently on those faults to which he was at last driven by that domestic infelicity which, to a delicate mind, is, of all evils, the most difficult to bear ; and, while we blame his errors, we cannot forbear to sympathize with his misfortunes. In short, his character, like that of all others, was of a mixed kind, but his good qualities far outweighed his defects.   W. G.

Kells Manse,
29th Juue, 1810.

Such is the valuable account of Lowe, given by Mr. Gillespie. The Editor will here shortly add what he was able himself to discover respecting the ballad of " Mary's Dream," among the peasantry of Galloway.

This ballad is extremely popular among them, but in a form materially different from the printed copy, long familiar to the public, which is entirely English. Their copy, if not altogether Scotch, is strongly sprinkled with it. But there is more than a mere difference of language; —it extends to the imagery and scenery of the poem. Was this ballad originally written in English by Lowe, and gradually converted by the country people into language and imagery more congenial to them ? Or was Lowe himself the author of both copies ; and if so, which is the original? This is a curious enquiry. Yet it is an enquiry which the Editor believes can lead but to one conclusion. He himself does not entertain a doubt that the Scotch copy is the original; but as the other has also its beauties, and has been long a favourite of the public, it would be charged upon him as presumption were he to exclude from this collection a ballad of such celebrity. He is induced therefore to insert here both the copies,

that the public may award to which of them the preference
is due.

MARY'S DREAM.

The moon had climb'd the highest hill,
  Which rises o'er the source of Dee,
And from the eastern summit shed
  Her silver light on tow'r and tree :
When Mary laid her down to sleep,
  Her thoughts on Sandy far at sea ;
When soft and low a voice was heard,
  Saying, Mary, weep no more for me.

She from her pillow gently rais'd
  Her head to ask who there might be ;
She saw young Sandy shiv'ring stand,
  With visage pale and hollow ee ;
" O Mary, dear, cold is my clay,
  It lies beneath a stormy sea ;
Far, far from thee I sleep in death ;
  So, Mary, weep no more for me.

" Three stormy nights and stormy days,
  We toss'd upon the raging main ;
And long we strove our bark to save,
  But all our striving was in vain.
E'en then, when horror chill'd my blood,
  My heart was fill'd with love for thee :
The storm is past, and I at rest ;
  So, Mary, weep no more for me.

O maiden dear, thyself prepare,
  We soon shall meet upon that shore,
Where love is free from doubt and care,
  And thou and I shall part no more !"
Loud crow'd the cock, the shadows fled,
  No more of Sandy could she see ;
But soft the passing spirit said,
  " Sweet Mary, weep no more for me !"

Old Way of "Mary's Dream."

The lovely moon had climbed the hill
Where eagles big* aboon the Dee,
And like the looks of a lovely dame,
Brought joy to every bodies ee ;
A' but sweet Mary, deep in sleep,
Her thoughts on Sandy far at sea ;
A voice drapt saftly on her ear,
" Sweet Mary, weep nae mair for me !"

She lifted up her waukening een,
To see from whence the voice might be,
And there she saw her Sandy stand,
Pale, bending on her his hollow ee !
" O Mary, dear, lament nae mair,
I'm in death's thraws† below the sea :
Thy weeping makes me sad in bliss,
" Sae, Mary, weep nae mair for me !"

" The wind slept when we left the bay,
But soon it waked and raised the main,
And God he bore us down the deep,
Who strave wi' him but strave in vain !
He stretched his arm, and took me up,
Tho' laith I was to gang but ‡ thee,
I look frae heaven aboon the storm,
" Sae, Mary, weep nae mair for me !"

" Take off thae bride sheets frae thy bed,
Which thou hast faulded down for me ;
Unrobe thee of thy earthly stole—
I'll meet wi' thee in heaven hie."
Three times the gray cock flapt his wing
To mark the morning lift her ee,
And thrice the passing spirit said,
" Sweet Mary, weep nae mair for me !"

---

*Build their nests.

† Thraws, throes.   ‡ But, without.

2 N

Here the Editor thinks, that whoever compares these
two copies together, cannot entertain a doubt that the
Scotch one is the original.   There is that freshness and
vividness of colouring in its sentiments and descriptions,
which uniformly characterize the genuine transcripts of
feeling ; and the scenery and imagery is such as a native
of Galloway, in the flow of inspiration, would be unavoid-
ably led to use.   In all these respects, it materially differs
from the printed copy, which, though very beautiful indeed, and certainly more uniformly correct, and higher
laboured than the other, contains a great deal less of the
simple language of the heart, and has no distinguishing
feature by which it can be attributed to the native of one
part of the island more than another.   To go no further
than the two opening lines, the English copy merely
describes the moon rising over a mountain, the source of
a river :

> " The moon had climb'd the highest hill
> Which rises o'er the source of Dee."

But in the other, we have the picture faithfully described, which was present to the poet's imagination :

> " The lovely moon had climbed the hill
> Where eagles big aboon the Dee."

We see here a Scotch landscape in all its characteristic
sublimity ;—the towering cliffs lost in the clouds, the
frightful abode of the eagle !

The two concluding lines of the first stanza in the English copy—

"When soft and low a voice was heard,
Saying, Mary, weep no more for me,"

are infinitely tamer and more prosaic than

"A voice drapt saftly on her ear,
Sweet Mary, weep nae mair for me !"

The omission of the word *saying*, in the Scotch, and bursting at once to the speech, has a happy effect.

How beautifully tender are the two following lines :

"Take aff thae bride sheets frae thy bed,
Which thou hast faulded down for me,"

and how cold and formal, in comparison, are the lines

"O maiden dear, thyself prepare," &c.

Every description seems, in a similar manner, to have lost what it had of picturesque effect in passing from Scotch to English. For instance, the crowing of the cock at the dawn of morning, is described in the following lines as a Shakespeare would have described it :

"Three times the gray cock flapt his wing,
To mark the morning lift her ee."

Here everything is in life and motion, fresh from a creative fancy ; but the daringness of fancy which dictated these lines, must have been long subdued, and succeeded

by very different emotions, before the same poet could
coldly write—

> " Loud crow'd the cock, the shadows fled." ˙

Every reader, of true poetical taste, must have felt the
bold sublimity and pathos of the whole of the third
stanza—

> " The wind slept," &c.

Here, in addition to the natural awfulness of the scene,
the poet has called to his aid whatever is most interesting
and majestic in religion.   There is a simple sublimity in
the lines—

> " And God he bore us down the deep,
> Who strave wi' him but strave in vain !
> He stretched his arm, and took me up,"

to which the Editor believes it would be doing an injury,
were he to compare it even to any thing of Burns.   It is
of a higher cast, and is more akin to the wild inspiration
of a Job or a David.   The struggles of suffering humanity, opposed to the arm of Omnipotence, present a con-
trast at which our faculties are lost in wonder and awe.
But even here, when his struggles are over, and when the
gates of bliss are opened to him, his affection remains un-
impaired.   All the happiness of heaven is insufficient to
make him forego his love ;—he enters it with reluctance

without her, and still watches over her with trembling solicitude.

> " He stretched his arm and took me up
> Tho' laith I was to gang but thee."

Madame Stael quotes, in *Corinne*, a thought of her father's, who represents it as an alleviation to a poor sinner, amidst all the torments of hell, that he caught an opening glimpse of heaven, when his beloved spouse was about to enter it. This thought has been very much admired ; but it appears strained and sought after when compared with the passage of the Scotch poet.

The reader will see that all these finely imagined circumstances do not appear in the English copy. When the ardour of the poet's mind had cooled, and he had to grope his way in a language not so familiar to him, they would appear to him of too bold a nature, and, on that account, no doubt have been suppressed.

It would be trespassing on the patience of the reader to enlarge on this subject. The Editor is conscious that he has already discussed it at too great a length ; but he hopes the enthusiasm which he feels for a beautiful poem will weigh with a generous public in his justification.

ImTheStory.com

Personalized Classic Books in many genre's

Unique gift for kids, partners, friends, colleagues

Customize:

- Character Names
- Upload your own front/back cover images (optional)
- Inscribe a personal message/dedication on the
  inside page (optional)

Customize many titles Including
- Alice in Wonderland
- Romeo and Juliet
- The Wizard of Oz
- A Christmas Carol
- Dracula
- Dr. Jekyll & Mr. Hyde
- And more...

Lightning Source UK Ltd.
Milton Keynes UK
UKOW030131240513

211160UK00004B/34/P